*Janice VanCleave's*

# Dinosaurs for
# Every Kid

## Other Titles of Interest from Wiley

*Janice VanCleave's*

# Dinosaurs for Every Kid

## Easy Activities that Make Learning Science Fun

**John Wiley & Sons, Inc.**
**New York • Chichester • Brisbane • Toronto • Singapore**

The publisher and the author have made every reasonable effort to insure that the experiments and activities in this book are safe when conducted as instructed but assume no responsibility for any damage caused or sustained while performing the experiments or activities in this book. Parents, guardians, and/or teachers should supervise young readers who undertake the experiments and activities in this book.

*Library of Congress Cataloging-in-Publication Data:*

VanCleave, Janice Pratt.
    [Dinosaurs for every kid]
    Janice VanCleave's dinosaurs for every kid : easy activities that
make learning science fun.
        p.     cm. — (Science for every kid series)
    ISBN 0-471-30813-7. — ISBN 0-471-30812-9 (paper)
    1. Dinosaurs—Experiments—Juvenile literature.    2. Science
projects—Juvenile literature.   [1. Dinosaurs.   2. Science
projects.]   I. Title.   II. Title: Dinosaurs for every kid.
III. Series: VanCleave, Janice Pratt.   Janice VanCleave Science for
every kid series.
QE862.D5V36   1994
567.9'1'078—dc20                                        93-28226

Printed in the United States of America

10 9 8 7 6 5 4 3 2 1

# Acknowledgments

I would like to thank my granddaughter, Lauren Russell, and her class at Bear Branch Elementary School for assisting me in testing the experiments in this book: Frankie Berg, Joel Burchfield, Barbara Byrd, Lindsay Canatrell, Cory Downing, Brandon Edgeworth, Rebekah Fontenot, Michelle Haskin, Derek Ladd, Maureen Haloney, Aramis McGinnis, Cindy Metcalfe, Shannon Montgomery, Matthew Passmore, Elizabeth Rogers, Lauren Russell, Ruth Ann Shirley, Spencer Smith, Dusty Smulik, Cody Spiva, Lacy Thomas, and Sabrina Wade. Other helpful testers were Gary and Rodney Giles, Ben, Bonnie, and Brett Parker.

A special note of thanks to their teacher, Mrs. Gracie Hancock, for directing the activities.

This book is dedicated to the San Jacinto Girl Scouts Daisy Troop # 10002.

Scout Leaders: Deborah Shirley and Ginger Russell
Scouts: Lindsey Davis, Michelle Haskin, Jessica Honsinger, Megan Marini, Sharron Montgomery, Heather Orth, Alex Rodriguez, Lauren Russell, Lindsy Sadowski, Ashley Shirley, Ruth Ann Shirley, Danae Smith, Britnee Stokes

# Contents

# Introduction

Studying dinosaurs is like stepping into a time machine and traveling back more than 65 million years. You have the opportunity to take a close-up peek at these amazing animals that no longer live on the earth. Scientists as well as laypersons, young and old, enjoy the mystery and excitement of discovering what these prehistoric animals looked like and how they behaved. Studying dinosaurs is also like reading the ultimate detective story. Many mysteries of the earth's past still lie buried, waiting for you or other scientific explorers to uncover and put together the puzzle pieces of fossil finds.

The thrilling part of studying dinosaurs is that there is so much more to be discovered, and that these discoveries will not necessarily be made by professional scientists. In fact, many of the major dinosaur fossils have been found accidentally by farmers in fields, or even by children. One such child was Mary Anning, an English girl who collected fossils along the beach as a hobby in the early 1800s. Mary's fascination for discovering fossils did not wane as she became an adult. One day, while waiting for her husband, Dr. Mantell, outside a patient's house, Mary found a large tooth. Her husband later identified it as being like a giant iguana tooth. They named the creature from which the tooth came *Iguanodon,* which means "iguana tooth."

The divisions of the earth's geologic time used in this book and in other books have been based on information shared by scientists from all the continents. It is this spirit of sharing that has provided a story of the earth's past. Each chapter of time has its own unique tale—and some are "told" only by the fossils. The reign of dinosaurs is one of these more interesting fossil tales.

People have many questions about dinosaurs, some of which scientists have answers for. This book will try to answer such puzzling questions as: Were dinosaurs good parents? How fast could they move? Did dinosaurs move in herds? Did they migrate? What color were dinosaurs? What caused their extinction?

This is a basic book about dinosaurs. It is designed to teach facts, concepts, and problem-solving strategies. The scientific concepts presented can be applied to many similar situations. The exercises, experiments, and other activities were selected for their ability to be explained in basic terms with little complexity. One of the main objectives of the book is to present the FUN of science.

## How to Use This Book

Read each chapter carefully and follow each procedure in order. We also suggest that you read the chapters in order because there is some development of information from the first to the last section. Each chapter includes the following information:

- The chapter subtitle identifies your goal for the chapter.
- **What You Need to Know:** A definition and explanation of facts you need to understand.
- **Exercises:** To help you apply the facts you have learned.
- **Activity:** A project related to the facts represented.
- **Solutions to Exercises:** With a step-by-step explanation of the thought process.

In addition, this book contains:

- **Appendix 1:** The first time a name of a dinosaur is introduced in the book it will be **boldfaced** followed by a phonetic spelling. All the dinosaur names and phonetic spellings are included in Appendix 1 with a brief description of each dinosaur.

- **Appendix 2:** A list of the Latin and Greek root words (and their meanings) that are used to name the dinosaurs.

- **Glossary:** The first time a term is introduced in the book it will be **boldfaced** and defined in the text. The term and definition are also included in the Glossary at the end of the book. Be sure to flip back to the Glossary as often as you need to, making each term part of your personal vocabulary.

- **More Books About Dinosaurs:** A bibliography of dinosaur reference books with a brief description of each.

## General Instructions for the Exercises

1. Read the exercise carefully. If you are not sure of the answers, reread What You Need to Know for clues.

2. Check your answers and evaluate your work.

3. Reread the exercise if any of your answers are incorrect.

## General Instructions for the Activities

1. Read each activity completely before starting.

2. Collect supplies. You will have less frustration and more fun if all the materials necessary for the activities are ready before you start. You lose your train of thought when you have to stop and search for supplies.

**3.** Do not rush through the activity. Follow each step very carefully, never skip steps, and do not add your own. Safety is of the utmost importance, and by reading each activity before starting, then following the instructions exactly, you can feel confident that no unexpected results will occur.

**4.** Observe. If your results are not the same as those described in the activity, carefully reread the instructions and start over from step 1.

# 1
# Buried Treasures

**What Fossils Are and
How They Are Formed**

## What You Need to Know

**Paleontologists** are scientists who study prehistoric life on earth. They do this by searching for **fossils** (traces of the remains of prehistoric animals and plants buried in the earth's crust); the word *fossil* comes from a Latin word meaning "to dig." The point where the fossils are located in the rock layers helps to determine the time period in which the organism lived. Lower layers of rock are usually older than upper layers, so fossils in these lower layers are considered to be from an earlier geologic time period. The fossils themselves reveal the kinds of plants and animals that occupied the earth during that period. Some of the oldest fossils are microscopic single-celled organisms and bacteria. These fossils give paleontologists clues as to the age of the earth, which is estimated to be about 4.5 billion years old.

Preserved remains of prehistoric organisms, such as bones or shells, are known as **body fossils**. Tracks, trails, burrows and other indirect evidence of prehistoric life are called **trace fossils**. Fossils are formed in different ways. Water containing minerals can seep into bones, slowly changing them to stone. When this happens to wood, the stone formed is called petrified wood. Some fossils are the actual remains of plants and animals preserved in **amber** (the hardened resin, or sap, from trees). This sticky liquid sometimes dripped to the ground, covering small organisms such as insects or spiders, or the organisms may have walked across the resin, become stuck, and sunk into it. When the resin hardened, it formed a long-lasting protective covering over the organisms. Another unusual type of burial occurred in tar pits such as the Rancho La Brea tar pits near Los Angeles. Animals trying to cross the pits became trapped and their remains sank into the thick, natural asphaltlike material. Their bones have been preserved by the tar.

Fossils are not always the actual remains of the living organism. Many fossils are just copies. Three methods of the formation of

fossil copies are imprints, molds, and casts. **Imprints** are impressions made by organisms in soft mud that were preserved when the mud solidified. Imprints can be traces of an animal's activity, rather than its actual remains. The hardened tracks of animals or the burrows of prehistoric worms in solidified mud are examples of fossil imprints.

**Molds** were made when organisms were totally or partially buried in mud that hardened into rock. Over time ground water dissolved the organisms, leaving cavities shaped like their bodies. Both imprints and molds are mirror images of the organisms.

If a mold was later filled with mud or mineral material, the filling hardened into what is called a **cast** (a reproduction that has the same outer shape as the organism). A cast looks like the organism itself, not like its imprint. Paleontologists make casts of fossil molds by filling them with liquids, such as plaster, that harden.

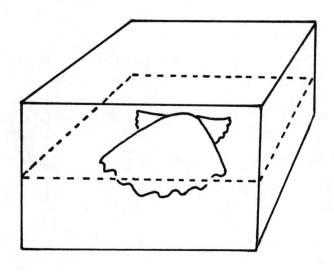

buried shell

## shell molds

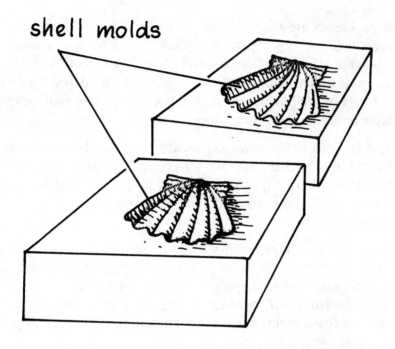

## Exercises

Study the diagrams on page 11 to answer the following questions:

1. Which of the two diagrams represents the first procedure in the formation of a trace fossil?

2. Which diagram represents the formation of a cast?

3. Which diagram is an example of the first procedure in the formation of a fossil imprint?

A

B

140 million years later

## Activity:  MAKING FOSSILS

**Purpose**  To demonstrate the formation of a fossil mold and cast.

**Materials**  modeling clay
paper plate
seashell (may be purchased at a crafts store)
petroleum jelly
7-oz (210-ml) paper cup
plastic spoon
plaster of paris
tap water

### Procedure

1. Take a piece of clay twice the size of the shell and squeeze it with your hands until the clay is soft and pliable.

2. Place the clay on the paper plate.

3. Coat one side of the seashell with petroleum jelly.

4. Press the lubricated side of the shell into the clay.

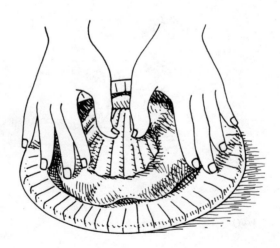

**5.** Carefully remove the shell from the clay.

**6.** Observe the imprint of the shell in the clay. Compare the imprint in the clay with the shape and texture of the outside of the shell.

**7.** In the paper cup, mix together 4 spoonfuls of plaster of paris with 2 spoonfuls of water.

**8.** Pour the plaster mixture into the shell imprint in the clay. NOTE: *Throw the cup and spoon away and do not wash any plaster down the sink as it can clog the drain.*

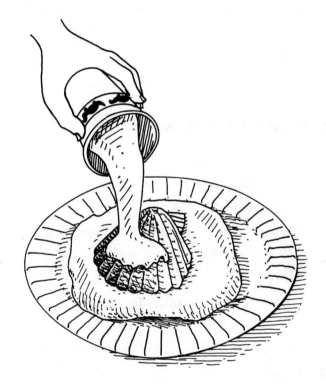

**9.** Allow the plaster to harden (about 20 minutes).

**10.** Gently separate the clay from the plaster.

**11.** Compare the shape and texture of the outside of the shell with the shape and texture of the outside of the plastercast.

**Results** The imprint of the shell in the clay and the outside of the shell are the same, but are mirror images. The outside of the shell and the plaster cast are identical.

**Why?** The imprint in the clay and the plaster cast are both examples of how fossils form. Pressing the shell into the clay represents burying the shell in mud. In nature, the mud would have hardened into rock around the shell. Removing the shell from the clay represents how the shell dissolves over long periods of time, leaving a cavity called a mold in the rock. The mold produced is a mirror-image imprint of the shell's outside surface. In nature this mold would have been filled with **sediment** (small particles of rock and mineral that are deposited by water, wind, or ice) that hardened into rock. The plaster of paris, like sediment, hardened but in a much shorter period of time. The plaster is a replica of the shell and is called a cast.

## Solutions to Exercises

1. *Think!*

   • What are trace fossils? The evidence of life such as tracks, trails, and burrows.

   *Diagram A represents the first procedure in the formation of a trace fossil.*

2. *Think!*

   • How is a cast formed? By filling a mold with a soft substance, such as mud or plaster, that hardens when dry.

   *Diagram B represents the formation of a cast.*

3. *Think!*

   • How were fossil imprints made? One way was that prehistoric animals left imprints of their feet as they walked through soft mud that hardened over time.

   *Diagram A is an example of the first procedure in the formation of a fossil imprint.*

# 2
# Drifters

## The Distribution of Dinosaur Fossils Around the Earth

## What You Need to Know

The distribution of different animal types throughout the world as a result of their natural movements is called **zoo-geography**. The zoogeography of **dinosaurs** (DIE-nuh-sawrs, extinct reptiles that lived about 65–225 million years ago), indicates that the continents were not always separated as they are today, but instead formed one large landmass. At first, many **geologists** (scientists who study the history of the earth) did not accept the idea of one large landmass.

In 1911 a German scientist, Alfred Wegener, was the first to propose the theory known as **continental drift**. This theory simply states that all the earth's landmasses were once a single body of land that separated over many millions of years and drifted apart to form what we now know as the continents. Much evidence from rocks and fossils has been found to support this theory. The shape of the continents today seem like huge jigsaw puzzle pieces that could fit together. And the facing edges of many continents have similar rock formations.

A very important piece of evidence to support the theory of continental drift is that fossils of the same dinosaurs and other kinds of living things have been found on different continents. Since the dinosaurs could not have swum across great oceans, many scientists believe this shows that these living creatures must have once been together on one landmass.

This huge landmass is known as **Pangaea**, which means "whole earth." The northern part of this giant continent was given the name Laurasia, and the southern part, Gondwanaland. You can see from the diagram on the next page how, prior to the separation of the continents, the dinosaurs could have roamed freely from one area to another.

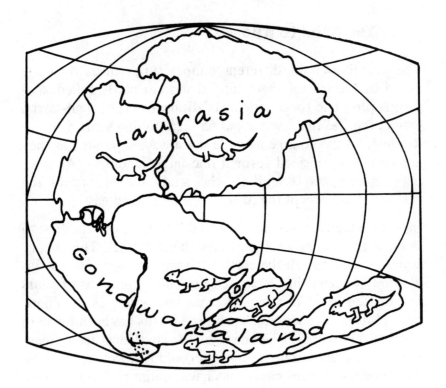

# PANGAEA

## Exercises

A very important find that gave support to Wegener's theory of continental drift was the discovery of the small hippopotamuslike reptile with a shovel-shaped jaw called **Lystrosaurus** (lie-struh-SAWR-us). Use the map showing the skulls of this ancient reptile to answer these questions:

1. Where did *Lystrosaurus* live on Pangaea?

2. In how many different areas of Pangaea is *Lystrosaurus* located?

3. Name two of the three continents (as we know them today) on which *Lystrosaurus* fossils have been found.

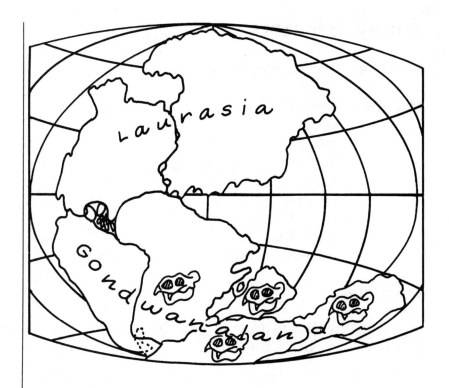

PANGAEA

Legend

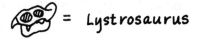 = Lystrosaurus

## Activity:  SPREADER

**Purpose**   To demonstrate continental drift

**Materials**   compass
pencil
ruler
1 sheet of typing paper
scissors
pie pan
tap water
toothpick
dishwashing liquid

## Procedure

1. Use the compass to draw a 4-inch (10-cm) diameter circle in the center of the paper.

2. Use the pencil and edge of the ruler to draw two intersecting lines, dividing the circle into four equal parts.

3. Draw a picture of the same dinosaur in each of the four sections.

4. Cut around the circle and along the lines to separate the four drawings.

5. Place the pie pan on a table and add enough water to cover the bottom of the pan.

6. Position the four pieces of paper as close together as possible to form a paper circle on the surface of the water.

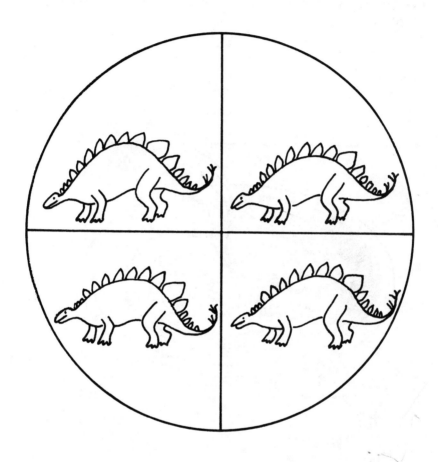

**7.** Wet one end of the toothpick with dishwashing liquid.

**8.** Put the wet end of the toothpick in the water in the center of the paper circle.

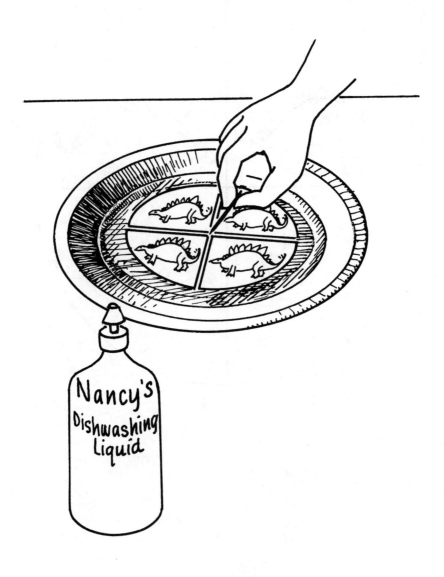

**Results** The paper pieces quickly move apart in all directions.

**Why?** The circle represents the single landmass that is believed to have existed during the age of the dinosaurs. The dinosaurs spread to different areas of the original landmass, then over millions of years, the land broke up into continents, separating the dinosaurs. The separating paper pieces can be compared to a film of time-lapse photography of the millions of years required for the landmasses of Pangaea to separate.

NOTE: *The paper pieces moved because the dishwashing liquid broke the surface tension of the water supporting the paper. For more information about surface tension see "Pepper Run" on page 170 of* Janice VanCleave's Physics for Every Kid *(New York: Wiley, 1991).*

## Solutions to Exercises

1. *Think!*

   • What is the name of the region of Pangaea where symbols for *Lystrosaurus* appear?

   Lystrosaurus *lived on Gondwanaland.*

2. *Think!*

   • How many symbols for *Lystrosaurus* appear on the map?

   Lystrosaurus *is located in four areas.*

3. *Think!*

   • Compare the map to a modern world map.

   • What modern continents look like the areas where *Lystrosaurus* fossils were found?

   Lystrosaurus *fossils have been found in Africa, Antarctica, Asia (China and India), and Australia.*

# 3
# Puzzle Pieces

## How Paleontologists Determine Facts About Dinosaurs from Fossil Remains

## What You Need to Know

From fossilized tracks, scientists can deduce many things about the size, speed, weight, and behavior of dinosaurs. Larger dinosaurs had longer legs and their footprints were farther apart. The depth of the tracks indicates how heavy the creature was. The deeper the track, the heavier the dinosaur. **Bipeds** (two-legged animals) were predominantly meat eaters, and **quadrupeds** (four-legged animals), with a few exceptions, ate plants. The bipedal prints are easily picked out by their pointed, three-toed, birdlike shape.

The number of prints found in an area provides evidence about dinosaur movements. **Tyrannosaurus rex** (tuh-RAN-uh-SAWR-us recks) may have traveled alone or in pairs, while **sauropods** (SAWR-uh-pods) formed herds and **Maiasaura** (mah-ee-ah-SAWR-uh) made nesting colonies where big groups of the animals came to lay eggs and to raise their young. The abundant number of bipedal footprints found running north-south along the eastern edge of the Rocky Mountains suggests that some dinosaurs migrated.

The fossil remains of a huge herd of Maiasaura were found in a layer of volcanic ash. The bones varied in size, and some scientists think that the herd was made up of babies, youngsters, teens, and adults. This further confirms that these and possibly other dinosaurs traveled in herds.

Dinosaur bones, like those of modern animals, had bumps where muscles were attached to the bones. Fossilized muscle tissue has been found on bones, but mostly it is the bones themselves that give clues to where muscles were attached. It is assumed that the skeleton and muscles of dinosaurs worked in a manner similar to that of modern animals. Thus, by studying modern animals, paleontologists can understand how dinosaurs looked and moved when they were alive.

Most dinosaur finds include just a few pieces of the skeleton, from which scientists try to piece together the rest of the animal, but occasionally a nearly complete skeleton is found. Paleontologists study the reconstructed skeletons of dinosaurs for clues. The skeleton of **Coelophysis** (see-luh-FYE-sis) gives an example of dinosaur detective work in action. The fossils of *Coelophysis* include sharp teeth with jagged edges, hands with fingers and sharp claws, and a slender body with hollow, lightweight bones. *Coelophysis* walked on two long, slim legs and its feet had strong, sharp claws. Scientists believe the claws and teeth were used to kill and eat prey. The lightweight bones suggest that it was probably a fast runner that ran down and killed its prey. The discovery of bones of whole families—from very young to adult animals—indicates *Coelophysis* gave some care to its young.

Often there aren't enough clues for scientists to draw one single conclusion. Scientists continue to look for answers to the many puzzling questions about dinosaurs.

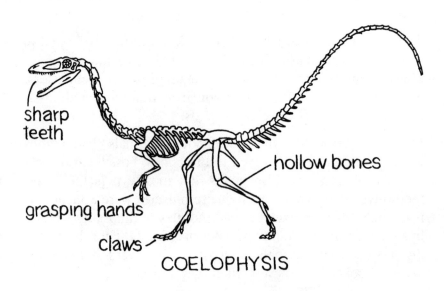

# Exercise

Scientists have found the tracks of the front feet of one quadrapedal dinosaur with only an occasional single print from one of its back feet. Study the two diagrams of an imaginary sauropod and choose the one that represents the more logical way that the prints may have been made.

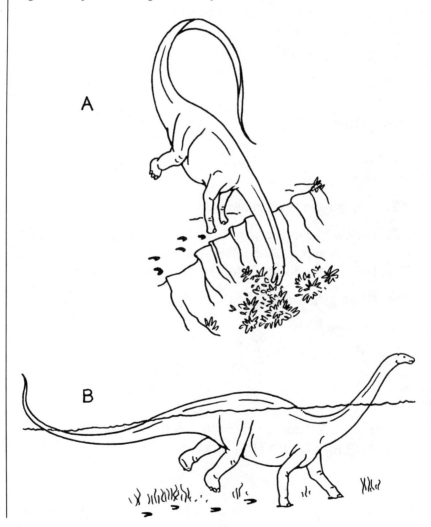

## Activity: DINOSAUR PUZZLE

**Purpose**  To represent the difficulty of identifying and assembling dinosaur bones.

**Materials**  ruler
marking pen
white poster board
scissors
2 paper lunch bags
timer
helper

## Procedure

1. Measure and draw two 6-by-6-inch (15-by-15-cm) squares on the poster board.

2. Cut out the two squares.

3. Follow the directions below to draw puzzle pieces on each of the squares. The directions refer to the lines by letters, but do not label the lines on your paper.

   ■ Line A: Draw a diagonal line across the paper.

   ■ Line B: Start at the bottom left corner of the paper and draw a 6-inch (15-cm) diagonal line.

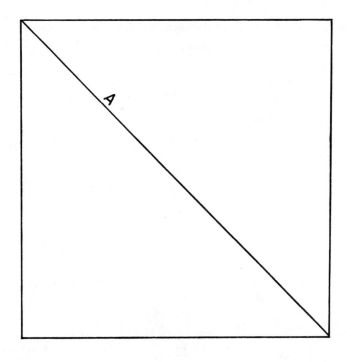

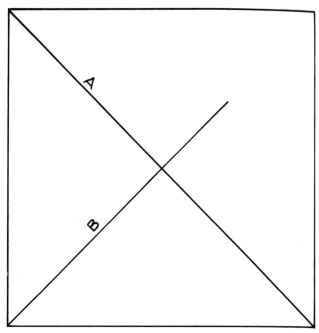

- Line C: Start at the end of line B and draw a line across the paper parallel to line A.

- Line D: Start where lines B and C meet. Draw a line between lines A and C that is parallel to the sides of the paper.

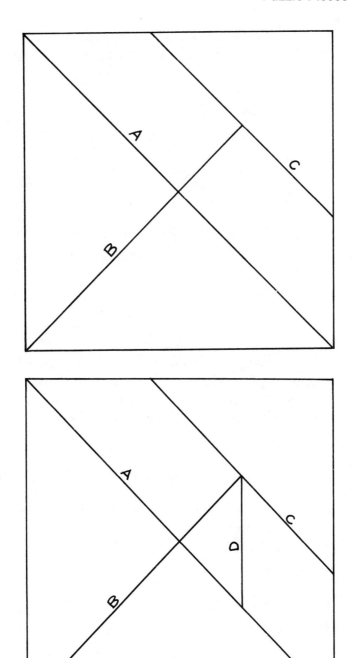

■ Line E: Start where line C touches the edge of the paper. Draw a line between lines A and C that is parallel to line B.

4. On the unruled side of one of the pieces of paper draw **Parasaurolophus** (PAR-uh-sawr-AHL-uh-fus), and on the unruled side of the other paper draw *Tyrannosaurus rex.* You may copy the drawings in this book.

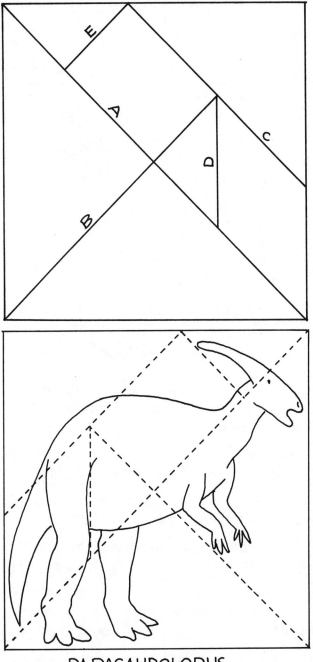

PARASAUROLOPUS

## TYRANNOSAURUS REX

**5.** Cut out the puzzle pieces of *Tyrannosaurus rex* and place them in one of the paper bags. Label the bag "Tyrannosaurus rex."

**6.** Cut out the *Parasaurolophus* puzzle, place the pieces in the other bag, and label it "Parasaurolophus."

**7.** Choose one of the bags. Shake it to mix the puzzle pieces inside, then pour the pieces onto a table.

**8.** Ask a helper to measure and record the time it takes you to arrange the puzzle pieces. Return the puzzle pieces to the bag.

**9.** Shake the second bag and ask your helper to measure and record the time it takes you to arrange these pieces.

**10.** Place the pieces of both puzzles in the same bag, and shake the bag to thoroughly mix the pieces.

**11.** Pour all the pieces onto the table and, as before, ask your helper to measure and record the time it takes you to arrange both of the puzzles.

**12.** Add the time needed to arrange the two puzzles individually and compare it to the time needed to arrange the mixed puzzles.

**Results** It usually takes longer to arrange the mixed puzzle pieces than to arrange the two puzzles individually.

**Why?** When the pieces of the two puzzles were mixed together, the pieces belonging to each puzzle had to be identified and separated before they could be arranged. This problem occurs when bones of different dinosaurs are found in the same area. Scientists must first identify the bones and then separate them before the bones can be assembled.

## Solution to Exercise

### Think!

- Is it likely that dinosaurs were able to stand on only their front feet as if doing a handstand? No, in fact it is not likely that they could balance on their front feet at all, thus diagram A is not a good solution.

- Could the dinosaur have been walking in water with only its front feet touching the bottom? Yes, in fact some scientists think the large sauropods walked on their front feet when walking through water deep enough to buoy up their rear ends. The single hind leg footprint among the foreleg footprints is thought to have been caused by the animal kicking with a back foot to change direction.

*Diagram B represents the more logical way that the prints may have been made.*

# 4
# The Ticking Clock

## Determining When Dinosaurs Roamed the Earth

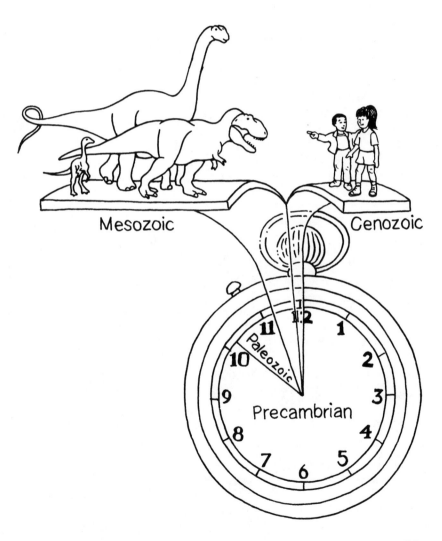

Mesozoic   Cenozoic

Paleozoic

Precambrian

## What You Need to Know

A **geologic time scale** is a chart that divides the history of the earth into units of time based on geologic changes in the earth's crust and sudden changes in life-forms, such as the disappearance of dinosaurs. With the help of fossils and rock layers, scientists have divided the history of the earth into four time intervals called **eras**. Major changes in the earth's crust and its life forms are used to determine eras.

The four eras of the earth's history are the Precambrian, Paleozoic, Mesozoic, and Cenozoic eras. From the beginning of time (4.5 billion years ago) to 600 million years ago was the first era in the geologic history of earth, the **Precambrian era**. Few fossils have been found to give clues about this long time span. More fossils have been found that indicate that life changed relatively fast from 600 million years ago to the present. This stretch of time is divided into three eras, referred to as ancient life, middle life, and recent life. The **Paleozoic era**, the oldest or "ancient life," started about 600 million years ago and lasted about 375 million years. In the early part of the era marine life was abundant because the seas covered large areas of the continents. By the end of the era, continental landmasses were no longer submerged, and land animals and plants increased in number. The **Mesozoic era**, "middle life," began about 225 million years ago and lasted about 160 million years. It is often called the Age of the Dinosaur because dinosaurs are believed to have lived during this time. The **Cenozoic era**, "recent life," is the time in which we presently live. This era began about 65 million years ago when the dinosaurs disappeared.

The beginning of any of the eras is not exact, but the beginning of the Precambrian era marks the creation of the earth.

Most scientists determine the age of the earth to be about 4.5 billion (4,500,000,000) years old, thus the Precambrian era started about 4.5 billion years ago. The clock in the diagram splits the history of earth's geologic time into the four eras so that you can compare the length of each era. If the earth's history were only 12 hours long, the Mesozoic era would have lasted only about 25 minutes.

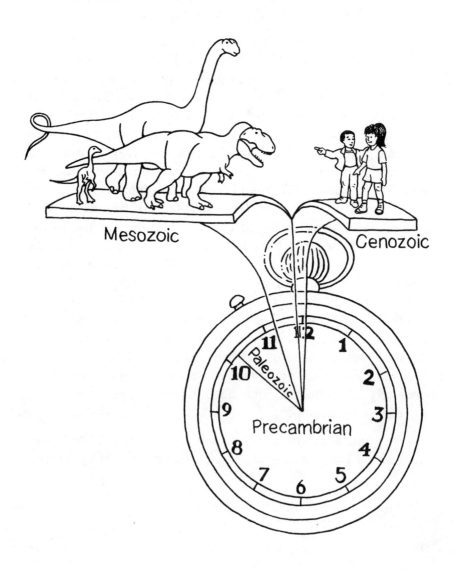

The Mesozoic era itself is divided into even shorter time intervals called **periods**. The three periods of this era are the **Triassic**, **Jurassic**, and **Cretaceous periods**. Fossil remains indicate that during the Triassic period the climate on the earth was dry and warm. A number of **Plateosaurus** (PLAY-tee-uh-SAWR-us) skeletons have been found that date back to the Triassic period, making this one of the oldest known dinosaurs.

From studying rock layers and fossil remains, scientists believe that during the early part of the Jurassic period the earth's surface was covered mostly by water. There are many remains of marine reptiles, including **Ichthyosaurus** (ICK-thee-uh-SAWR-us) and **Plesiosaurus** (PLEE-zee-uh-SAWR-us), found in Jurassic rock layers. Many of the largest dinosaur fossils, such as **Brachiosaurus** (BREAK-ee-uh-SAWR-us) and "**Supersaurus**" (su-per-SAWR-us), have been found in Late Jurassic rock.

The last of the three periods of the Mesozoic era is the Cretaceous period. Plant life is believed to have been very abundant in the Cretaceous period. The number of dinosaur species began to decline in the latter part of the period, and by the end of the period, all the dinosaurs had become extinct. Scientists are still trying to figure out why. Most dinosaur fossils have been found in Late Cretaceous rock layers. The chart on the next page shows the order of the periods of the Mesozoic era and the duration of each.

# Age of the Dinosaur

| Era | Period | Time (years ago) |
|---|---|---|
| M e s o z o i c | Cretaceous | 65 million ↓ 135 million |
|  | Jurassic | ↓ 195 million |
|  | Triassic | ↓ 225 million |

## Exercises

Use the Dinosaur History showing representative dinosaurs of each period of the Mesozoic era to answer the following questions:

1. Which of the dinosaurs represented lived during the earliest period?

2. Which of the dinosaurs lived here fewer than 135 million years ago?

3. **Stegosaurus** (steg-uh-SAWR-us) lived during what era and period?

# Dinosaur History

| Era | Period | Age (years ago) | Kind of Dinosaur |
|---|---|---|---|
| Mesozoic | Cretaceous | 65 million<br><br>Late<br><br><br>Early<br><br>135 million | Triceratops<br>Tyrannosaurus rex |
| Mesozoic | Jurassic | Late<br><br><br>Early<br><br>195 million | Stegosaurus<br>Brachiosaurus |
| Mesozoic | Triassic | Late<br><br>Early<br>225 million | Plateosaurus |

## Activity:   TIME LINE

**Purpose**   To construct a scale model of the earth's geologic eras.

**Materials**   meterstick
scissors
adding machine tape
masking tape
pencil

## Procedure

1. Measure and cut a 460-cm piece of adding machine tape.

2. Stretch the paper strip out on an uncarpeted floor and use tape to secure the ends.

3. Draw a line across the tape 5 cm from the top. Print "Present" above this line.

4. Draw a second line 6.5 cm from the first line. Label this line "65 million" and write "(65)" vertically on the right side of the tape in this section.

5. Draw a third line 16 cm from the second line. Label the line "225 million" and write "(160)" on the right side as in the previous step.

6. Draw a fourth line 37.5 cm below the third line. Label the line "600 million" and write "(375)" on the right side as before.

7. Print "Beginning" at the bottom of the tape. Write "4,500 million" above the word and "(3,900)" on the side.

8. Use the diagram to label these eras on the tape "Cenozoic," "Mesozoic," "Paleozoic," and "Precambrian."

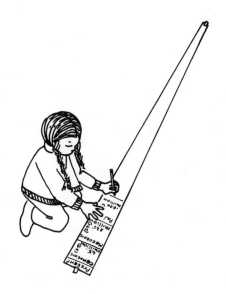

| Present | |
| :---: | :---: |
| Cenozoic<br>65 million | (65) |
| Mesozoic<br><br>225 million | (160) |
| Paleozoic<br><br>600 million | (375) |
| Precambrian<br><br><br>4,500 million<br>Beginning | (3,900) |

**Results**   A time line comparing the length of time of the four different geologic eras of the earth's history is constructed.

**Why?**   The paper scale uses length to compare the differences in time between the earth's four geologic eras. The length of the eras can be compared at a glance by studying the size of each section. A more accurate length of time for each era appears in the numbers along the side. The shortest and the youngest section is the Cenozoic era, which so far has lasted about 65 million years. The era of the dinosaurs is second in age and lasted for about 160 million years. The eras preceding the Mesozoic era increase in length of age, with the Precambrian era being the largest section, the longest era, and the oldest era.

## Solutions to Exercises

1. *Think!*

    • Look at the age of each period. Which period occurred longest ago? Triassic.

    • What dinosaur lived during the Triassic period?

    Plateosaurus *is the dinosaur that lived during the earliest period.*

2. *Think!*

    • Which dinosaurs are shown above the 135-million-year age line?

    **Triceratops** (try-SAIR-uh-tops) *and* Tyrannosaurus rex *lived here fewer than 135 million years ago.*

3. *Think!*

    • Find *Stegosaurus* on the chart. Place your finger on the drawing and move your finger to the left until it is in the column labeled "Period." What name appears in this column? Jurassic.

- Move your finger to the column labeled "Era." What name appears in this column? Mesozoic.

Stegosaurus *lived during the Mesozoic era and the Jurassic period.*

# 5
# How Old?

## Determining the Relative Age of Dinosaurs

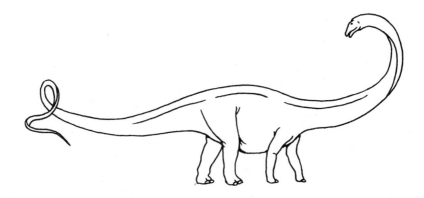

## What You Need to Know

Fossils of dinosaurs are often found by people other than paleontologists. Rock collectors, miners, and construction workers sometimes uncover fossils while digging. Before the 19th century little importance was given to fossils. Around 1815 an English engineer and scientist, William Smith, realized that certain varieties of fossils were found only in certain layers of rock. He also observed that if a layer of rock containing one type of fossil occurred on top of a layer containing a different type of fossil in the same location, then the fossil layers occurred in the same order wherever they were found together. This observation and the understanding that the bottom layers were formed first gave scientists a means of constructing a geologic history of the earth in which events can be placed in proper order of age.

young

medium

old

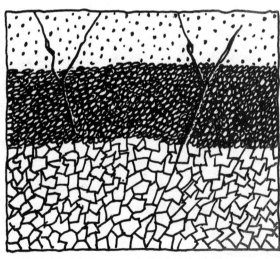

The **relative age** of an object or event is its age as compared with that of another object or event. Finding the relative age simply places things in order of occurrence. In a group of rock layers, the bottom layer is usually the oldest and the top layer the youngest. Generally, each layer is younger than the one beneath it and older than the one above it, except when the earth has been moved through natural or man-made events.

The relative age of a rock layer indicates the relative age of the dinosaur fossils found in the rock. To say that **Diplodocus** (die-PLOD-uh-cus) is older than *Triceratops* but younger than *Coelophysis* is to give the relative age of *Diplodocus*. The relative age of *Diplodocus* is determined by the location of its fossils in relationship to the location of other fossils. For example, fossils from *Diplodocus* have been found in rock layers sandwiched between layers containing *Coelophysis* and *Triceratops*. *Coelophysis* fossils, being the oldest, have been found in lower layers, and *Triceratops* fossils, being the youngest, have been **excavated** (dug out and removed from the earth) from an upper rock layer.

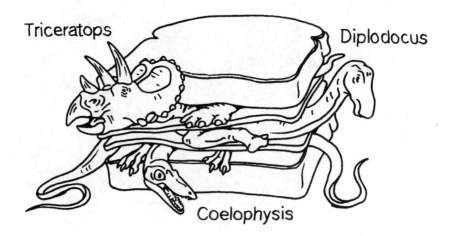

Triceratops   Diplodocus

Coelophysis

## Exercises

The Mesozoic era is called the Age of the Dinosaur. Scientists have divided this age into three periods, as shown in the diagram. Use the diagram and the legend to answer the following questions:

**1.** Is *Coelophysis* older or younger than *Tyrannosaurus rex*?

**2.** Which two dinosaurs in the diagram are the youngest and are about the same relative age?

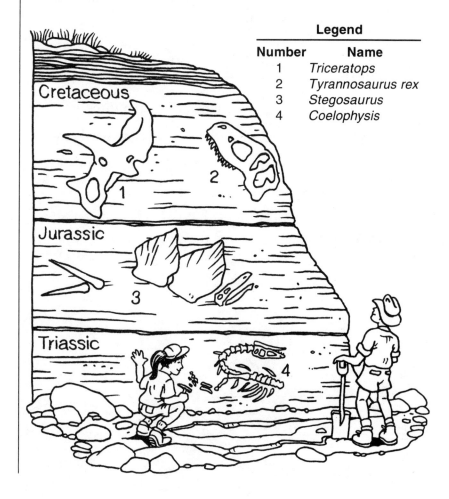

| Legend | |
|---|---|
| **Number** | **Name** |
| 1 | *Triceratops* |
| 2 | *Tyrannosaurus rex* |
| 3 | *Stegosaurus* |
| 4 | *Coelophysis* |

## Activity: LAYERING

**Purpose**  To simulate how deposited sediments form layers in the bottom of a lake.

**Materials**  ½ cup (125 ml) each of 3 different colors of
          aquarium gravel
          3 bowls
          1½ cups (375 ml) soil or sand
          spoon
          2-quart (2-liter) rectangular glass baking dish
          tap water
          timer

### Procedure

**1.** Pour one color of gravel into each of the three bowls.

**2.** Add ½ cup (125 ml) of soil or sand to each bowl of gravel.

**3.** Use the spoon to mix the gravel and soil thoroughly.

**4.** Fill the baking dish halfway with water.

**5.** Use your hand to slowly sprinkle the gravel-soil mixture from one of the bowls into the water.

6. Wait 10 minutes and observe the appearance of the layer formed by the mixture.

7. Sprinkle the gravel-soil mixture from one of the remaining bowls into the water.

8. Again wait 10 minutes and observe the appearance of the materials in the dish.

9. Add the last gravel-soil mixture.

10. After 10 minutes observe the contents of the dish.

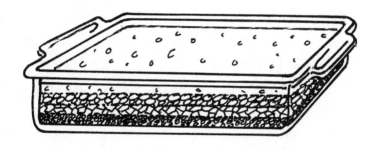

**Results** The three different colored mixtures form separate layers in the dish.

**Why?** The gravel and soil that make up the sediment sank through the water to form layers. Because the mixtures of gravel and soil were added at 10-minute intervals, the bottom layer is relatively older and the top layer is relatively younger than the other layers. Layers of rock are believed to form in a similar manner, and like the gravel-soil mixture, each rock layer is laid down on top of the one beneath it. This is how scientists can tell the relative age of each layer.

## Solutions to Exercises

### 1. *Think!*

- What are the legend numbers for *Coelophysis* and *Tyrannosaurus rex?* 4 and 2.

- Find the two legend numbers in the diagram. What is the order of the numbers in the layers of rocks? 4 is below 2.

- If the fossils of *Coelophysis* are found below those of Tyrannosaurus rex, which of the two is older?

Coelophysis *is older than* Tyrannosaurus rex.

### 2. *Think!*

- Which layer contains the youngest fossils? The top Cretaceous layer.

- Which fossil bones, as identified in the legend, are found in the Cretaceous layer of rock?

Tyrannosaurus rex *and* Triceratops *are the youngest and are about the same relative age.*

# 6
# Breakdown

## Determining the Age of
## Dinosaur Bones and Other Fossils

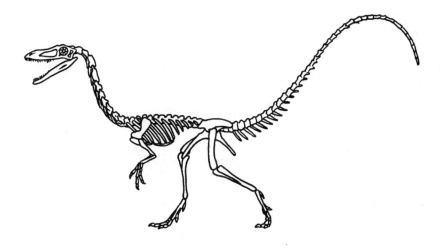

## What You Need to Know

Most dinosaur bones were buried in sediment. Over long periods of time the sediment and the bones turned to rock. Some of the fossilized bones contain special elements that are **radioactive**, that is, they have undergone internal nuclear change or decay. This type of decay is different from a chemical decay of material, such as the rotting of meat. When meat rots or decays, atoms that are combined within the meat move apart and then recombine in different ways. In **radioactive decay**, the atom releases **radiation** (a form of energy) from its **nucleus** (center of the atom) and creates an atom of another element.

Potassium is an example of a radioactive substance. K-40 is the identifying symbol for radioactive potassium. When K-40 decays it changes into argon 40 (Ar-40). The decay of K-40 is a slow process that occurs over many years. In fact, it takes about 1.3 billion years for half of a **mass** (the amount of matter contained in a substance) of K-40 to change into Ar-40. The time it takes for half of the mass of a radioactive material to decay is called the **half-life.** The material continues to decay until there is nothing left to decay.

For example, suppose a rock contained 100 grams of K-40. After 1.3 billion years, half of the 100 grams of K-40 would change into Ar-40. Thus, the rock would then contain 50 grams of K-40 and 50 grams of Ar-40. The radioactive potassium would continue to decay, and at the end of a second 1.3 billion years half of the remaining 50 grams of K-40 would have changed to Ar-40, leaving 25 grams of K-40 and adding another 25 grams of Ar-40 to the rock. The rock would then contain 25 grams of K-40 and 75 grams of Ar-40.

# RADIOACTIVE DECAY

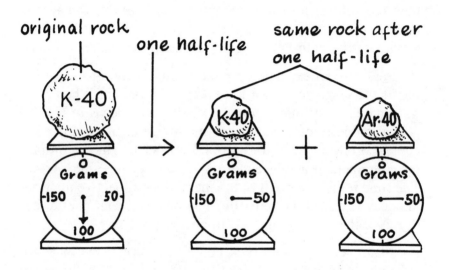

original rock

one half-life

same rock after
one half-life

This process would continue until there were no more K-40 atoms to change to Ar-40 atoms.

The age of rocks and fossils can be determined by comparing the amount of its unchanged radioactive element with that of its decay product. For example, if equal amounts of K-40 and Ar-40 are found, it would mean that half of the K-40 has decayed, making the age of the material equal to one half-life of K-40, or 1.3 billion years.

## Exercises

**1.** Radioactive elements other than K-40 are also used to date rocks and fossils. Use the chart of some of the radioactive elements used in dating rocks and fossils and their estimated half-lives to answer the following questions:

**a.** If a rock was found containing 25 grams of rubidium 87 (Rb-87) and 25 grams of strontium 87 (Sr-87), how old would the rock be?

**b.** How many years does it take for carbon 14 to go through two half-lives?

### RADIOACTIVE ELEMENTS USED IN DATING

| Element | Decay Product | Estimated Half-Life (in years) |
|---------|---------------|--------------------------------|
| rubidium 87 (Rb-87) | strontium 87 (Sr-87) | 500 billion |
| thorium 232 (Th-232) | lead 08 (Pb-08) | 14.1 billion |
| carbon 14 (C-14) | nitrogen 14 (N-14) | 5,730 |

**2.** Use the bar graph showing the radioactive decay of 100 grams of uranium 238 (U-238) to answer these questions:

**a.** What is the half-life of U-238?

**b.** If a rock contained 100 grams of U-238, how many grams of U-238 would be left in the rock after 9 billion years?

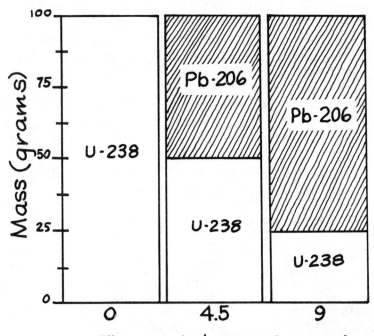

RADIOACTIVE DECAY OF U-238

## Activity:  HEADS UP

**Purpose**   To simulate radioactive decay and the dating of a fossilized bone.

**Materials**   hand towel
masking tape
marking pen
bowl
small empty coffee can with a lid
100 pennies
timer

### Procedure

**1.** Stretch the towel out on a table.

**2.** Use the tape and marking pen to label the bowl "Changed" and the can "Unchanged."

**3.** Place all of the coins in the can.

**4.** Set the timer for 1 minute.

**5.** At the end of 1 minute, pour the coins out of the can and onto the towel. (The towel keeps the coins from rolling off the table.)

**6.** Transfer half of the coins to the bowl. Record this as being the first division.

**7.** Return the remaining coins on the towel to the can.

**8.** Again set the timer for 1 minute.

**9.** Continue to separate the coins at the end of each minute, keeping track of how many divisions are made. Stop when the number of coins is so small that you cannot divide it (when only one coin remains in the can). Record this as being the last division. NOTE: *When trying to divide odd numbers, such as 25 coins, place the closest even number back into the can. For 25 coins, return 12 coins to the can.*

**10.** Each division of the coins represents one half-life of a ra-dioactive element. How many half-lives are represented?

**Results**   The coins are divided seven times. Thus, seven half-lives are represented.

**Why?**   The time it takes for half of a radioactive element to change to another element is called its half-life. The half-life in this activity was 1 minute. At the end of 1 minute, half of the coins were placed in the bowl (changed) to demonstrate the change that occurs in radioactive elements. After another minute, half of the remaining coins were placed in the bowl, leaving only one-fourth, or 25 coins, in the can (unchanged) and a total of 75 coins in the bowl. As time passed, the number of coins in the bowl increased, but the number of coins in the can decreased, just as all radioactive elements will eventually change. In reality, it usually takes thousands, millions, and even billions of years for the change to occur.

## Solutions to Exercises

### 1a. *Think!*

- How does the mass of Rb-87 compare to that of Sr-87? Their masses are equal.

- Equal masses of a radioactive element and its decay product indicate that a period of time equal to one half-life has passed.

- What is the half-life of Rb-87?

*The rock would be 500 billion years old.*

### b. *Think!*

- What is the length of one half-life of C-14? 5,730 years.

- What would be the length of two half-lives? 2 × 5,730 years.

*It would take C-14 11,460 years to go through two half-lives.*

### 2a. *Think!*

- Which period of time shows equal amounts of U-238 and its decay product, Lead 206 (Pb-206)?

*The half-life of U-238 is 4.5 billion years.*

## b. *Think!*

- Find the bar above 9 billion years and place your finger on the line above the U-238 section of the bar.

- Move your finger to the left until it touches the mass scale of the graph. What mass reading does your finger touch?

*25 grams of U-238 would be left in the rock after 9 billion years.*

# 7
# What's in a Name?

**Learning About the Meanings
of the Names Given to Dinosaurs**

## What You Need to Know

The names of dinosaurs are made up of combinations of Latin and Greek root words to describe facts about the animal, such as its believed appearance and behavior. Other parts of the names may include where the dinosaur was discovered or even the name of the scientist who made the discovery. The word *dinosaur* derives from *dino,* meaning "terrible," and *saur,* meaning "lizard."

Some names are relatively short, such as **Ankylosaurus** (ang-kih-luh-SAWR-us), while others are real tongue twisters, such as **Micropachycephalosaurus** (MY-kro-PACK-ee-SEF-uh-luh-SAWR-us). A short list of Greek and Latin root words is given in the following chart on the next page. (NOTE: *A more complete list can be found in Appendix 2.* ) To figure out what the name of a dinosaur means, follow the procedure below:

### Steps to Understanding Dinosaur Names

**1.** Write the name correctly: "Ankylosaurus."

**2.** Find the root word *ankylo* and write down its meaning: "crooked."

3. Find the root word *saurus* and write down its meaning: "lizard."

4. Combine the meanings of the root words to discover the meaning of the name *Ankylosaurus*: "crooked lizard."

### DINOSAUR NAME CHART

| Name | Meaning | Name | Meaning |
|------|---------|------|---------|
| ankylo | crooked | mega | large |
| anuro | no tail | micro | small |
| bary | heavy | pachy | thick |
| brachio | arm | pod | foot |
| cephalo | head | rex | king |
| ceros | horn | saur, saurus | lizard |
| compso | pretty | tri | three |
| di | two | tyranno | tyrant |
| dino | terrible | veloci | speedy |
| masso | bulk, body | | |

## Exercises

Use the Dinosaur Name Chart to answer the following questions:

1. What does the tongue-twisting name *Micropachycephalosaurus* mean?

2. What kind of dinosaur is described by the fictitious name *Dicerosmegapodsaurus* (di-SAIR-us-MEG-uh-pod-SAWR-us)?

3. Draw an imaginary dinosaur that the fictitious name *Compsobarymassosaurus* (KOMP-so-BARE-ee-MASS-uh-SAWR-us) describes.

## Activity: THE NAME GAME

**Purpose**   To draw imaginary dinosaur shapes and give them descriptive names.

**Materials**   6 unruled index cards
            pencil

## Procedure

1. Number and lay three of the index cards side by side on a table.

2. Draw your own imaginary dinosaur across the three cards. Use the diagram as a guide to place the tail on card 1, the body and limbs of the animal on card 2, and the neck and head on card 3.

3. Remove card 3 with the neck and head of the animal and replace it with a blank card (card 4).

4. Draw a differently shaped neck and head on card 4 by extending the lines from card 2.

5. Remove card 2 and replace it with card 5.

6. Draw a differently shaped body on card 5 by extending the lines from the cards on the left and the right.

7. Remove card 1 and replace it with a blank card (card 6).

8. Draw a differently shaped tail by extending the lines from card 5.

9. Rearrange the six cards to construct dinosaurs of different shapes.

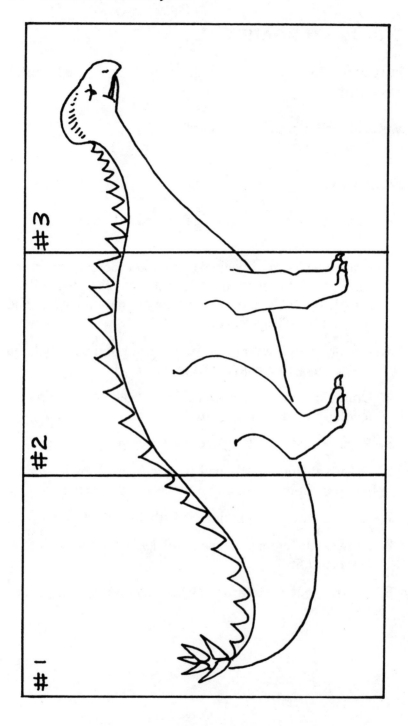

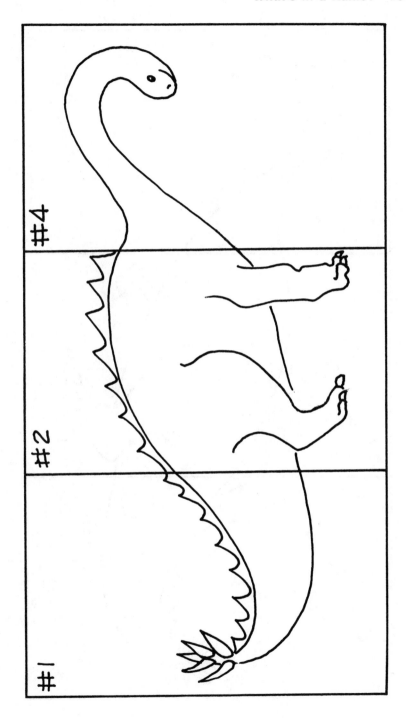

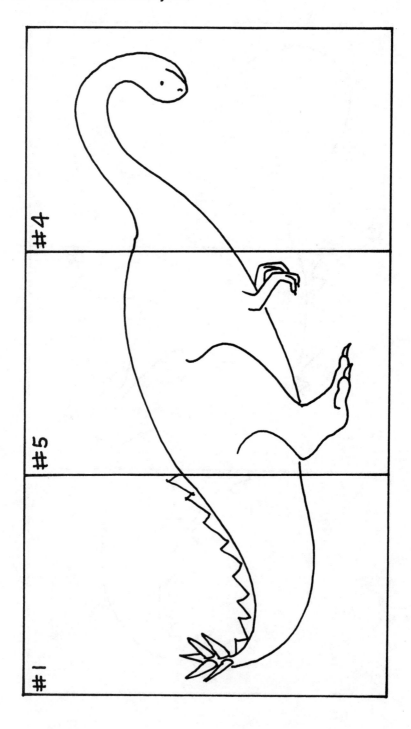

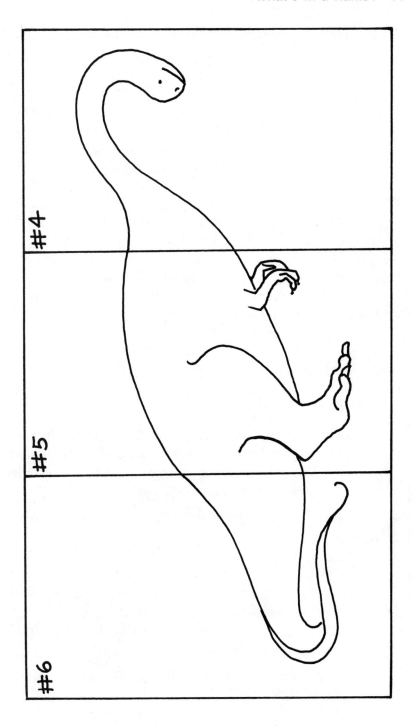

**10.** Use the Dinosaur Name Chart in this chapter or Appendix 2 to name each of the dinosaurs.

**Results**   Six interchangeable cards with dinosaur body parts are made. The cards can be rearranged to produce imaginary dinosaurs with differently shaped tails, bodies, and necks and heads. The names given to each dinosaur can vary depending on the drawing and on the person doing the naming.

**Why?**   The lines drawn on the cards meet when the cards are placed side by side, allowing you to create different dinosaur shapes. The names of dinosaurs can describe what they look like, how you believe they behaved, where they were discovered, or the name of the person who discovered them. The only restriction in naming a dinosaur is not to give it a name that has already been used.

## Solutions to Exercises

### 1. *Think!*

- Break the name *Micropachycephalosaurus* into its root words and find the meaning of each in the Dinosaur Name Chart: micro (small), pachy (thick), cephalo (head), and saurus (lizard).

*The name* Micropachycephalosaurus *means "small, thick-headed lizard."*

### 2. *Think!*

- Break the name *Dicerosmegapodsaurus* into its root words and find the meaning of each in the Dinosaur Name Chart: di (two), ceros (horn), mega (large), pod (foot), and saurus (lizard).

*The name* Dicerosmegapodsaurus *describes a two-horned, large-footed lizard.*

## 3. *Think!*

- What is the description of a dinosaur named *Compsobarymassosaurus*? The root words mean

  | compso | bary | masso | saurus |
  |--------|------|-------|--------|
  | (pretty) | (heavy) | (body) | (lizard) |

*The name* Compsobarymassosaurus *describes a pretty, heavy-bodied lizard.*

NOTE: *The diagram shows the author's idea of what this imaginary dinosaur might look like.*

COMPOBARYMASSOSAURUS

# 8
# Tiny to King-Size
## The Different Sizes of Dinosaurs

## What You Need to Know

The word *dinosaur* conjures up thoughts of unbelievably huge animals—taller than many multistory buildings. Some adult dinosaurs were in fact taller than five-story buildings, but some were about the size of a chicken. The length of adult dinosaurs ranged from about 2 feet (60 cm) to about 100 feet (30 m).

One of the tiniest dinosaurs known was **Compsognathus** (komp-so-NAY-thus). This meat-eating dinosaur was no bigger than a modern chicken. It is believed that even when fully grown this small dinosaur weighed only about as much as a newborn human baby.

Most of the dinosaurs were much larger than the tiny *Compsognathus,* but adult *Triceratops* and *Tyrannosaurus* might be considered of an average size. *Triceratops* was about 30 feet (9 m) long, 9.5 feet (2.9 m) tall, and weighed 6 tons (5.4 metric tons). *Tyrannosaurus rex* was about 50 feet (15 m) long, 20 feet

Tyrannosaurus rex     African elephant

(6 m) tall, and weighed about the same as a modern African elephant, 6 tons (5.4 metric tons).

A king-size dinosaur given the name **Ultrasaurus** (ul-truh-SAWR-us) was discovered in Colorado in 1979 by James Jensen. This specimen is the largest dinosaur that has been excavated to date. This enlarged *Brachiosaurus*-shaped dinosaur is believed to have been the length of three school buses and the height of a six-story building, and to have weighed more than 20 elephants.

## Exercise

At the end of each path is a description of the dinosaur on that path. Trace the paths with your finger to match the drawing of each dinosaur with its description.

APATOSAURUS
(uh-PAT-uh-SAWR-us)
Height: 15 feet (4.5 m)
Length: 70 feet (20 m)
Weight: 30 tons
  (27 metric tons)

KRITOSAURUS
(KRIT-uh-SAWR-us)
Height: 15 feet (4.5 m)
Length: 30 feet (9 m)
Weight: 3 tons
  (2.7 metric tons)

DRYOSAURUS
(DRY-uh-SAWR-us
Height: 4 feet (1.2 m)
Length: 12 feet (3.5 m)
Weight: 170 pounds (77 kg)

## Activity: BODY SUPPORTERS

**Purpose** To build a *Cubeosaurus,* an imaginary dinosaur, and test the supportive ability of two differently shaped legs and a tail.

**Materials** 1 sheet of typing paper
pencil
scissors
transparent tape
modeling clay

### Procedure

1. Lay the sheet of typing paper over the *Cubeosaurus* patterns.

2. Carefully trace each pattern onto the paper.

3. Cut each pattern piece out of the paper.

4. Fold the body of the *Cubeosaurus* along the lines marked "fold." NOTE: *All folds should be made in the same direction on each pattern piece.*

5. Use tape to secure the tab sections, forming a cube for the body.

6. Fold the straight legs along the lines marked "fold" and tape the top of the legs to the bottom of the body.

7. Fold the arms along the line marked "fold" and tape them to the sides of the body.

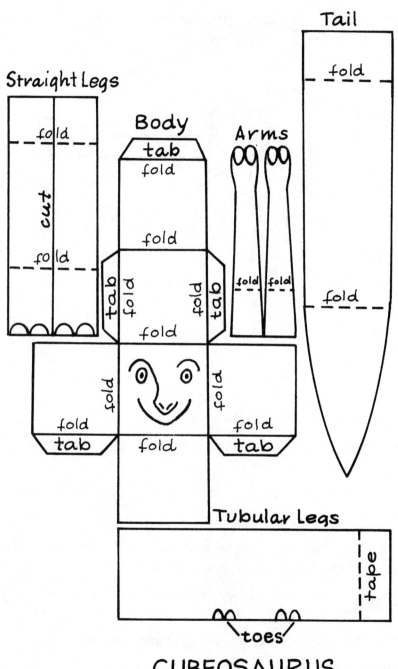

Tail

Straight Legs

Body

Arms

fold

tab
fold

fold

cut

fold

fold

tab
fold
fold

fold
tab

fold

fold

fold

fold
tab

fold

fold
tab

fold

Tubular Legs

toes

tape

CUBEOSAURUS

8. Fold the tail and tape the squared-off end to the back of the body (the side opposite the face).

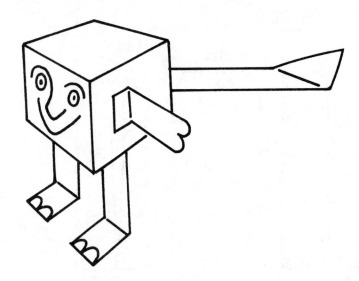

9. Stand *Cubeosaurus* on a flat surface.

10. Place a small marble-size piece of clay on top of the *Cubeosaurus's* body.

11. Continue to add clay pieces until the model collapses.

12. Remove and save the clay pieces.

13. Make the tubular leg set by rolling the pattern, securing it with tape, and standing it on end.

14. Remove the straight legs and stand the *Cubeosaurus* body on the tubular leg set.

15. Place the clay pieces used previously on top of the model.

16. Observe the effect of the extra weight of the clay on the tubular legs.

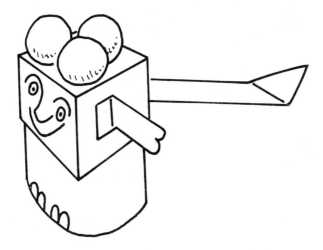

**Results**   A three-dimensional paper model of an imaginary dinosaur is made. Adding weight to the model causes the straight legs and tail to bend and collapse. The tail and tubular leg set are able to support the added weight.

**Why?**   With the aid of the tail, the thin, straight legs were able to support the paper model, but as extra weight was added, the straight legs and tail bent under pressure. The tubular set represented extra-strong leg bones, like those of elephants, which were able to support more of the dinosaur's weight. This is why the largest dinosaurs had thick, strong legs.

## Solution to Exercise

### *Think!*

• Where do the paths lead for each of the dinosaurs?

*Dinosaur A:* Apatosaurus.

*Dinosaur B:* Kritosaurus.

*Dinosaur C:* Dryosaurus.

# 9
# Modeling

## How Scientists Determine the Weight of Dinosaurs

## What You Need to Know

The size of dinosaur fossils leads scientists to believe that the weight of these animals was many times greater than the largest animals on earth today. Edwin H. Colbert, an American paleontologist, devised a method to determine the weight of dinosaurs. Colbert's procedure requires that a scale model of the dinosaur be made. The scientist must decide on the scale; for example, 1:20 means that the original dinosaur was 20 times larger than the scale model. Muscle scars on the bones are used as guides to determine the amount of muscle and other tissue the dinosaur probably had.

The volume of a clay scale model can be found by placing the model in a container and filling the container with dry sand. The dinosaur model is then lifted out of the container and is replaced with additional sand until the container is filled. The number of quarts (liters) of additional sand is equal to the volume of the model dinosaur. The volume of the actual dinosaur is calculated by multiplying the volume of the model by the scale used.

Next, the scientist relates the volume of the dinosaur to its weight. The volume and weight of a modern alligator are used to relate volume to weight because scientists assume that the composition of dinosaur and alligator bodies are similar. This comparison is estimated to be about 2 pounds of weight per quart of volume (0.9 kg per liter).

By using this method, scientists have determined the weight of *Brachiosaurus*, at 80–100 tons (72–90 metric tons), to be many times that of *Diplodocus* weighing about 12 tons (10.8 metric tons). The weight of *Diplodocus* was unexpectedly small since the bodies of both dinosaurs were about the same length. The difference in weight is because *Diplodocus's* length was mostly in its tail. Most of *Brachiosaurus's* length was in its body and legs, so overall it weighed more.

DIPLODOCUS

BRACHIOSAURUS

## Exercise

*Stegosaurus* was not large compared to most dinosaurs. Assume that Colbert's method was used to determine the weight of this modest-size dinosaur. With the data listed below, calculate the weight of *Stegosaurus*.

### DATA

**a.** A scale of 1:20 was used to make a model of the dinosaur.

**b.** One hundred quarts (liters) of replacement sand was needed to fill the space left when the dinosaur model was removed.

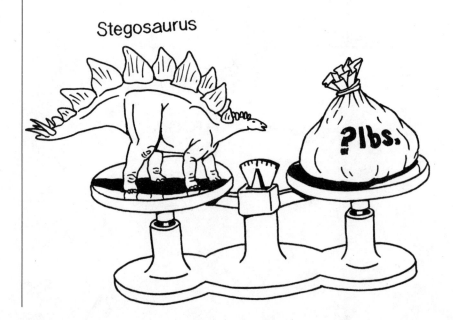

Stegosaurus

## Activity:   REDUCED MODEL

**Purpose**   To make a 1:8 scale model of *Compsognathus* and determine its weight.

**Materials**   mixing bowl
2 cups (500 ml) table salt
1 cup (250 ml) flour
¾ cup (188 ml) tap water
spoon
eyedropper
3 drops cooking oil
measuring cup (250 ml)
1-gallon (4-liter) plastic pail
sand

### Procedure

**1.** Make a batch of modeling clay by following the steps below:

- Mix together the salt and flour in the bowl.

- Slowly add the water as you stir.

- Use the eyedropper to add the oil.

- Stir well.

**2.** Use 2 cups (500 ml) of clay and the diagram to make a model of *Compsognathus*. Make sure your model will fit inside the pail.

## COMPSOGNATHUS MODEL

**3.** Allow the model to dry. This may take two or more days, depending on the thickness of the model and the humidity.

**4.** Stand the model in the pail.

**5.** Fill the pail with sand.

**6.** Gently remove the model from the pail and shake off any sand that sticks to the model.

**7.** Use the measuring cup to measure and add sand to the pail. Record the amount of sand needed to refill the pail as the replacement volume of sand.

**8.** Determine the weight of the actual *Compsognathus* by using the replacement volume of sand, the scale of the model (1:8), and the weight scale of 2 pounds per quart (0.9 kg per liter).

**Results**   The replacement volume of sand needed to fill the pail after the small, birdlike model is removed is equal to the amount of clay used which was 2 cups (500 ml) or ½ quart (liter). The weight of the actual dinosaur was calculated to be 8 pounds (3.6 kg).

**Why?**   The model displaced ½ quart (liter) of sand. This quantity of sand is equal to the volume of the model. The 1:8 scale used in constructing the model indicates that the actual dinosaur was eight times as large as the model. The weight of the actual *Compsognathus* that the clay figure is modeled after is calculated using the following procedure:

**1.** Calculate the volume of the actual dinosaur by multiplying the volume of the model by the scale:
½ quart (liter) $\times$ 8 = 4 quarts (liters).

**2.** Multiply the volume of the actual dinosaur by the comparison of volume and weight determined for dinosaurs (2 pounds per quart, 0.9 kg per liter):
4 quarts (liters) $\times$ 2 pounds per quart (0.9 kg per liter) = 8 pounds (3.6 kg).

At about 8 pounds (3.6 kg), *Compsognathus* was one of the smallest dinosaurs. This animal was about the size of a large chicken.

## Solution to Exercise

### Think!

• How many replacement quarts (liters) of sand were needed? 100 quarts (liters).

• How much replacement sand would have been needed had the actual dinosaur been covered in sand? Since the actual dinosaur is 20 times larger than the model, the volume of

100 **Dinosaurs for Every Kid**

the dinosaur would have been 100 quarts (liters) × 20 or 2,000 quarts (liters).

- What is the comparison between weight and volume of dinosaurs? For every 1 quart (liter) of volume, the dinosaur weighed 2 pounds (0.9 kg). Thus, the weight of an actual *Stegosaurus* is equal to the volume times 2 pounds (0.9 kg):
2,000 quarts (liters) × 2 pounds per quart (0.9 kg per liter).

Stegosaurus *weighed 4,000 pounds (1,800 kg).*

# 10
# Outer Coverings
## Theories About the
## Type and Color of Dinosaur Skin

## What You Need to Know

There are many theories about the types of skin that dinosaurs most likely had. Sometimes fossil imprints give clues to the texture of the skin of a few dinosaurs, such as **Anatosaurus** (uh-NAT-uh-SAWR-us). Scientists know more about this duckbilled dinosaur than other dinosaur because of the many skeletons and skin imprints that have been found. Its skin had a rough, pebbly texture. The bumps were similar to those found on the skin of a present-day Gila monster. The fossil imprints of the skin of other dinosaurs indicate different types of skin textures, such as granular scales like those found on modern lizards, or heavy, bony armor plates embedded in the skin.

There are many theories, but no proof, that dinosaurs had colored skin. It is possible that, like modern animals, dinosaurs used color as an attention-getter during courtship, a means to frighten off possible attackers, or **camouflage** (a disguise caused by similarities between the colors and/or patterns of an animal's body and its environment). Because color pigments are not usually found in fossils, scientists have always thought that dinosaurs were dull in color, possibly gray like elephants and rhinos, or dull green or brown like crocodiles and alligators. Recently, however, a fossilized turtle shell with red coloring was found, giving scientists hope that a well-preserved dinosaur skin with coloring will be found.

## Exercises

Match each animal on page 102 to one of the three **habitats** (the place where an animal or plant naturally lives or grows).

1. Babies of many modern animals are born with spots or stripes. If the baby remains still on the ground, its spots or stripes act as camouflage. Baby dinosaurs also may have been protected by this type of camouflage. Choose the most protective habitat for the baby dinosaur.

2. Many land animals today have a dark back and a pale belly. From a distance and in bright open spaces, this type of shading makes it difficult for enemies to see them. Choose the habitat that *Brachiosaurus* would be least likely to stand out in.

Habitat A

Habitat B

Habitat C

## Activity:  **HIDING OUT**

**Purpose**  To demonstrate camouflage with color and patterns.

**Materials**  1 sheet of tracing paper
pencil
scissors
8 sheets of construction paper: 2 green,
    1 yellow, 1 orange, 1 white, 1 black, 1 red,
    1 brown
glue stick

## Procedure

**1.** Lay the tracing paper over the patterns for the tree trunk and leaf.

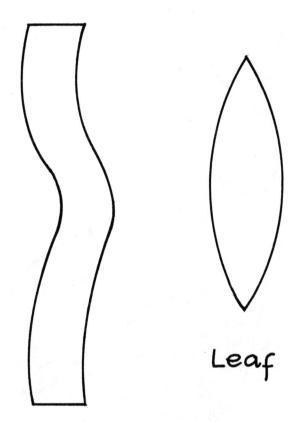

Leaf

# Tree Trunk

**2.** Trace and cut out both pattern pieces.

**3.** Lay the two sheets of green paper aside and fold the remaining pieces of construction paper in quarters.

**4.** Place the leaf pattern near the edge of one sheet of the folded paper.

**5.** Trace around the outside of the pattern. You should be able to trace six leaves on each of the yellow, orange, white, black, and red papers.

**6.** Cut out each leaf, making sure to cut through all four layers of paper for each of the five sheets of paper. You will have 24 leaves of each color.

**7.** Place the tree trunk pattern on the folded sheet of brown paper.

**8.** Draw around the outside of the tree trunk pattern three times and cut around each, cutting through all four layers of paper. You will have 12 brown tree trunks.

**9.** Glue six of the tree trunks on each sheet of green paper, as shown in the diagram.

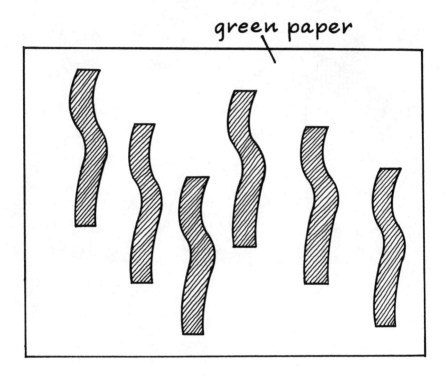

**10.** Glue an equal number of leaves of each color over the trunks on both sheets of green paper. Cut some of the leaves in half and glue them along the bottom edge of each sheet to form colored grass.

**11.** Turn over *one* of the pictures and draw a dinosaur on the back.

**12.** Cut out the dinosaur.

**13.** Place the dinosaur, green side up, on the uncut picture of
the trees. Observe how well you can see the dinosaur.

**14.** Turn the dinosaur over, multicolored side up, and place it on the uncut picture of the trees. Again observe how well you can see the dinosaur.

**Results** The green dinosaur is more visible than the multicolored dinosaur.

**Why?** The multicolored dinosaur blends in with the colors of the background. The yellow on the dinosaur blends in with the yellow leaves on the tree, and your eye is not sensitive enough to tell them apart. This happens with each of the colors. An animal whose coloration is similar to that of its environment is often camouflaged from predators. The stalking animal's eyes cannot distinguish between the colors enough to see its meal among the leaves.

# Solutions to Exercises

## 1. *Think!*

- Which habitat has a color or pattern most similar to that on the baby dinosaur's body?

*Habitat B is the most protective habitat for the baby dinosaur.*

## 2. *Think!*

- Where could a four-story dinosaur hide? It is hard to imagine an animal of this size being inconspicuous, but in an open space the animal is more difficult to see from a distance.

- Which habitat appears to be the most open?

Brachiosaurus *is least likely to stand out in Habitat C.*

# 11
# Overlapping
## Learning About Dinosaur Vision from Fossils

## What You Need to Know

The size of the eye sockets in the skull of a dinosaur tells scientists how large the animal's eyes were, which gives clues to the quality of the animal's vision. Generally, the larger the eyes, the better the vision. The fossil skulls of *Anatosaurus* have large eye sockets and marks on the fossil indicate well-developed optic nerves. These fossil clues tell scientists that *Anatosaurus* had a keen sense of sight. Both plant- and meat-eating dinosaurs needed good vision to find their food and protect themselves from predators.

Another important clue about the vision of dinosaurs comes from the position of their eyes. Eyes in the front of the skull rather than on the side focus together on an object and perceive it as a single three-dimensional image. The spacing of the eyes also affects the ability of the animal to judge distances. Dinosaurs with eyes facing forward on the front of their heads, such as the **Troödon** (troe-o-don), may have had vision much like your own, which is better for judging distances than are eyes on each side of the head. With forward-facing eyes, the dinosaur viewed objects from two different

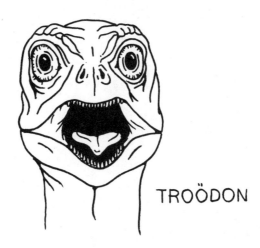

TROÖDON

angles. The two images were projected on the **retina** (the back layer of the eyeball, where images are focused by the eye's lens), where they overlapped. The overlapping images were interpreted by the animal's brain as one clear three-dimensional picture. This ability to combine into one picture the images viewed by two eyes is called **binocular vision**.

The long neck of some of the dinosaurs like that of *Plateosaurus* further assisted them in viewing the world around them. They could easily turn their heads to get a 360-degree view, while short-necked dinosaurs had to turn their bodies to see the same panoramic view.

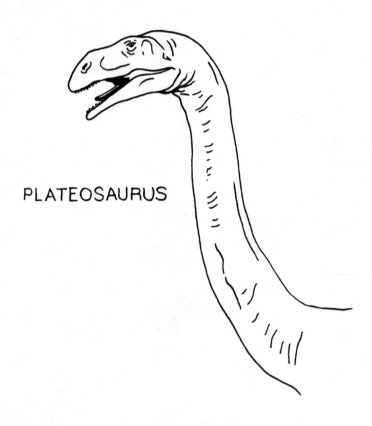

PLATEOSAURUS

## Paleontologist's Toolbox:   VISION SCALE

**Materials**   1 sheet of tracing paper
ruler
pencil
scissors

### Procedure

**1.** Fold the tracing paper in half so that the two short ends meet.

**2.** Place the end of the ruler in one corner of the folded edge.

**3.** Make a pencil mark along the open edge of the paper 4 inches (10 cm) from the corner.

**4.** Rotate the ruler as shown in the diagram to make 7 or 8 marks, all 4 inches (10 cm) from the corner.

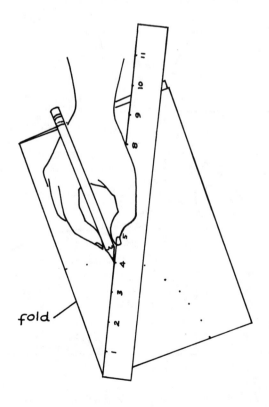

**5.** Draw a line to connect the marks.

**6.** Cut through both layers of paper along the line.

**7.** Unfold the paper and make a dot in the fold along the straight edge of the paper.

**8.** Label the tool "Vision Scale."

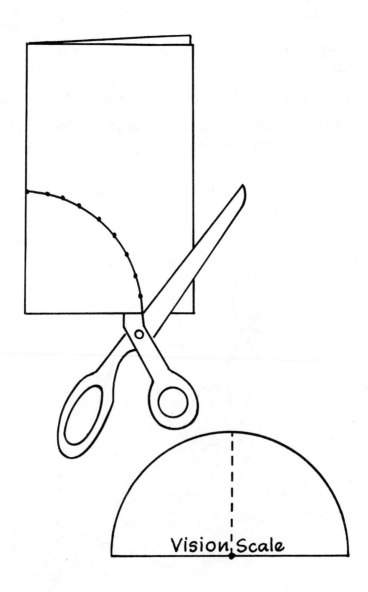

# Exercise

Some dinosaurs had about the same **peripheral vision** (what can be seen to the sides while looking straight ahead) as other animals whose eyes face forward (including you!). In the diagram *Pattysaurus* is trying to sneak past her friend, *Johnnysaurus*. Follow the instructions on page 120 to use your vision scale to determine when *Johnnysaurus* can first see *Pattysaurus* with his peripheral vision.

Place the vision scale on the diagram so that its bottom edge lines up with *Johnnysaurus'* eyes and the center mark points toward his nose. The area within the arc is his field of vision. Which stone is the first within his field of vision?

## Activity: FIELD OF VISION

**Purpose** To determine the field of vision of a dinosaur's eyes.

**Materials**   poster board
pencil
washer
string
2 crayons: 1 yellow, 1 blue
helper

## Procedure

1. Place the poster board on the floor.

2. Stand on the poster board with your feet together in the center of one long edge.

3. Ask your helper to draw an outline around your feet and to make a mark along the edge of the poster board between your heels.

4. Raise your left arm to the side until it is level with your shoulder.

5. Ask your helper to tie the washer to the end of the string and loop enough of the string over the upper part of your outstretched arm so that the washer hangs just above the poster board.

NOTE: *Keep your head and your eyes pointing straight ahead during steps 6–13.*

**6.** Close your right eye and, with your head held still, slowly move your outstretched left arm backward or forward until your open eye can no longer see your fingertips.

**7.** Ask your helper to make a mark on the poster board directly underneath the hanging washer. Label the mark "left."

8. Raise your right arm to the side until it is level with your shoulder, and ask your helper to transfer the string to the right arm. Lower your left arm.

9. Keep your right eye closed and, with your head held still, slowly move your outstretched right arm *forward* until you can see your fingertips.

10. Again ask your helper to make a mark on the poster board directly underneath the hanging washer. Label the mark "left."

11. Repeat steps 4–10 with your left eye closed. Label each mark "right."

12. Step off the paper and draw lines to connect the marks and show the fields of vision of the left and right eyes, as shown in the diagram.

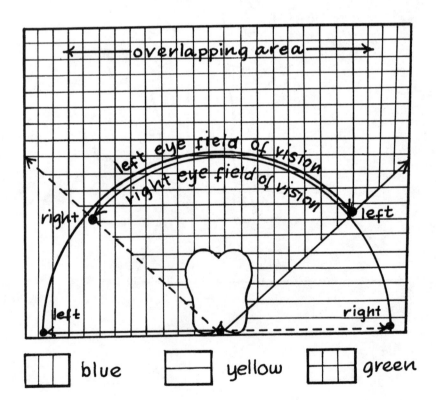

**13.** Color the field of vision for the left eye blue.

**14.** Color the field of vision for the right eye yellow.

**Results** The fields of vision of the left and right eyes are equal and they overlap, as shown by the greenish color in the center of your diagram.

**Why?** The entire field of vision when both eyes are open and facing forward is about 180 degrees. The fossil skull of the *Troödon* shows that, like humans, its eyes faced forward and were spaced apart. This spacing of the eyes causes the fields of vision of the left and right eyes to overlap, producing three-dimensional vision. This type of binocular vision was important to dinosaurs like *Troödon* and other dinosaurs believed to be active predators.

## Solution to Exercise

### *Think!*

• Follow the straight edge of the vision scale out to the stepping stones.

• Which stone is first within *Johnnysaurus's* field of vision?

Johnnysaurus *can first see* Pattysaurus *with his peripheral vision when she steps on Stone C.*

# 12
# What's for Dinner?

## How to Distinguish Plant-Eating from Meat-Eating Dinosaurs

## What You Need to Know

Dinosaurs or any animals that eat mainly plants, such as modern horses and cows, are called **herbivores**. Animals that eat mainly meat are called **carnivores**. There may have been more herbivorous than carnivorous dinosaurs. Fossil remains of dinosaurs give paleontologists clues that enable them to determine the diet of dinosaurs. Occasionally, the fossilized remains of a dinosaur's stomach contents are found, but more often it is other clues that determine the dinosaurs preferred food. Some of these clues include the shape of teeth, and the shape and number of feet the dinosaur walks on. Strong, flat, grinding teeth suggest herbivorous animals. Although there are exceptions, dinosaurs that walked on four feet usually were herbivores. Carnivorous dinosaurs as a rule walked on two feet that were three-toed and pointed like bird feet. They had large, sharp teeth and powerful jaws. Some dinosaurs such as *Anatosaurus* could have a thousand or more teeth in their mouths at one time.

**Chasmosaurus** (kaz-muh-SAWR-us) and **Opisthocoelicau-dia** (o-PISS-thuh-SEE-luh-CAW-dee-uh) were typical herbi-vores. *Chasmosaurus* and *Opisthocoelicaudia* both lived in the Late Cretaceous period, but because of the difference in body structure they did not compete for the same food. *Chasmo-saurus* most likely used its parrotlike beak to cut through tough plant stems of ground plants, while *Opisthocoelicaudia*, with its long neck, roamed the forest nipping off the branches of trees. These animals and others like them spent most of their waking hours munching on plants. They ate many times their own weight in food each year.

*Tyrannosaurus rex* is a typical example of a carnivore. It had the largest of any dinosaur teeth found, which were about 6 inches (15 cm) long. These long, knifelike teeth had jagged edges that could cut into meat like steak knives.

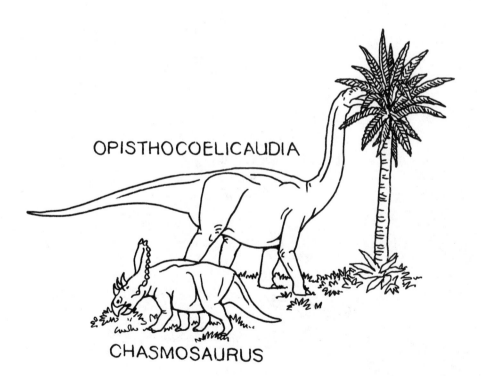

OPISTHOCOELICAUDIA

CHASMOSAURUS

## Exercises

Use your detective skills to identify these dinosaur skulls as herbivores or carnivores.

**1.** *Maiasaura* was a duckbilled dinosaur with rows of short, flat teeth on both upper and lower jaws.

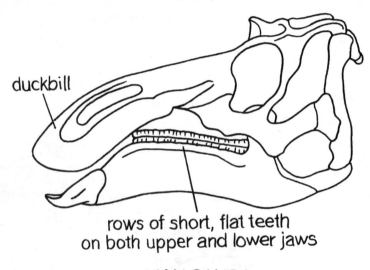

duckbill

rows of short, flat teeth
on both upper and lower jaws

MAIASAURA

**2.** All of *Coelophysis's* teeth are sharp with jagged edges.

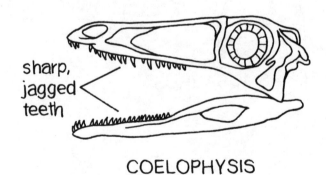

sharp,
jagged
teeth

COELOPHYSIS

**3.** *Triceratops* had rows of short, flat teeth on both sides of its mouth and a long, sharp beak.

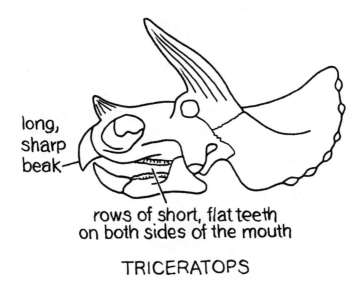

long,
sharp
beak

rows of short, flat teeth
on both sides of the mouth

TRICERATOPS

## Activity: GRINDERS

**Purpose**  To determine how dinosaurs without grinding teeth ate their food.

**Materials**  20 green leaves from a large tree or bush—ask an adult to select the leaves
2 resealable plastic bags
5 walnut-size rocks

## Procedure

**1.** Observe the shape of the leaves and then place 10 leaves in each plastic bag.

**2.** Add the rocks to one of the bags of leaves.

**3.** Hold the bag of leaves that do not contain the rocks between the palms of your hands.

4. Rub your hands together vigorously against the plastic bag 25 times.

5. Open the bag and remove the leaves.

6. Observe the shape of the leaves.

7. Hold between the palms of your hands the bag of leaves that contains the rocks.

8. Rub your hands together vigorously 25 times as before. NOTE: *Do not rub so hard that you injure your hands.*

9. Remove the leaves and observe.

**Results**  The shape of the leaves in the bag that does not contain the rocks changes slightly or not at all. The leaves in the bag that contained the rocks were crushed.

**Why?**  Some dinosaurs, like *Apatosaurus,* had long, thin teeth at the front of extended jaws. These teeth could have been used to rake in leaves, but were not useful for chewing. *Apatosaurus* and other dinosaurs with a similar body makeup probably did not chew their food, but swallowed it whole. Paleontologists have found large polished rocks near the rib bones of *Apatosaurus* fossils. The location of these stones suggests that they were swallowed, just as modern chickens swallow gravel and use it to grind food inside their bodies. The food inside the dinosaur's body was pulverized by the rocks as the rocks moved around, just as the leaves were ground by the rocks in the bag.

## Solutions to Exercises

### 1. *Think!*

- What kind of teeth does the *Maiasaura* skull contain? Short teeth in the back of its jaw.

- Could these teeth be used to attack and tear into animal flesh? No. Short, flat teeth were more useful in chewing plant fiber.

Maiasaura *was a herbivore.*

### 2. *Think!*

- Describe the teeth in the *Coelophysis* skull. Sharp, jagged, or sawlike.

- Are these the type of teeth used to chew plants? No, they are used like a steak knife to slice through meat.

Coelophysis *was a carnivore.*

## 3. *Think!*

- How is the *Triceratops* skull different from the other two: It has a sharp beak.

- What kind of teeth does the *Triceratops* skull contain? Short, flat teeth.

- What use would the beak and short, flat teeth have? The sharp beak could cut through strong stems of plants, and the rows of short, flat teeth could chew tough plant leaves that other dinosaurs could not eat.

Triceratops *was a herbivore.*

# 13
# Tails Up
## The Uses of Dinosaur Tails

## What You Need to Know

The tails of dinosaurs were reptilian-like, but varied in length and thickness. The use of the tail depended on its size and shape, as well as the physical structure of the dinosaur. Some bipeds, such as **Hypsilophodon** (hip-sih-LOF-uh-don), had rodlike tendons that lay along each side of the tail vertebrae. These supportive tendons are believed to have held the tail out rigidly, which allowed the tail to act as a counterbalance when the animal ran.

HYPSOLOPHODON

Tails like that of **Iguanodon** (ih-GWAHN-uh-don) may have been used as a brace to support the animal as it stood upright, possibly reaching up to tear leaves and twigs off trees. Other bipeds had tails like those of modern alligators—slender and long, tapering down to the tip. These tails would have been useful when swimming.

IGUANODON

The tails of quadrupedal dinosaurs varied greatly in length. Quadrupeds built like *Diplodocus* needed long tails to counterbalance the weight of their very long necks. These long tails may also have been used like a whip to drive off threatening predators. Other dinosaurs, such as *Triceratops,* resembled modern rhinoceroses and they possibly moved like rhinoceroses. Their tails, though short compared to those of *Diplodocus,* were thick and heavy. Dinosaurs with a body structure like that of *Triceratops* did not need a long tail for balance to walk and run.

The use of the tail as a defensive weapon seems most likely for dinosaurs similar to *Stegosaurus,* whose tail had spikes on the end, or **Minmi** (MIN-my), an armored dinosaur with protective bony plates on its body and tail. *Ankylosaurus* was another armor-covered dinosaur, but its tail looked even more threatening with a bony club on its tip. The muscles in the hind legs and tails of animals like these were very strong, allowing the animals to turn around, swinging their tails with enough force to wound a predator.

Scientists do not agree on how the dinosaurs with long tails carried their tails—whether the tails were held up or dragged on the ground. A puzzling fact is that drag marks of tails are seldom found with most dinosaur tracks.

## Exercise

The dinosaurs pictured here appear to be having problems. And no wonder! Their tails have been switched. Match up each dinosaur body (indicated by letter) with its correct tail (indicated by number).

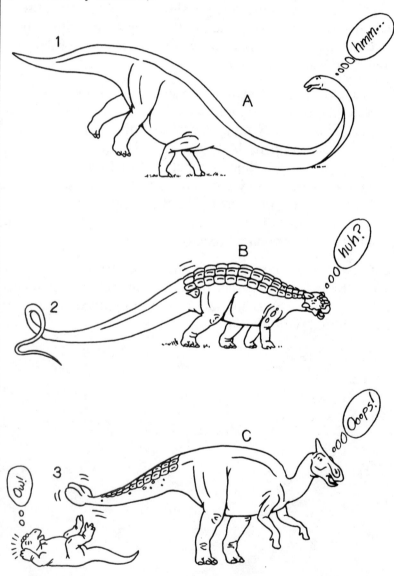

## Activity: TRAILERS

**Purpose**   To demonstrate how a sauropod's long tail counterbalanced its long neck.

**Materials**   scissors
ruler
1 unruled index card
marking pen
drinking straw
transparent tape
8-inch (20-cm) piece of 20-gauge insulated wire
4 washers
modeling clay
pencil

## Procedure

1. Cut out a 2-by-1-inch (5-by-2.5-cm) section from the index card.

2. Copy the drawing of a *sauropod's* body (shown here) on this section of the card, and turn the card face down.

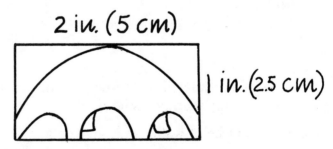

2 in. (5 cm)

1 in. (2.5 cm)

3. Cut a 2-inch (5-cm) section of straw.

4. Tape the straw along the bottom of the card.

5. Thread the piece of wire through the section of straw so that an equal amount of wire extends from each end of the straw.

**6.** Bend the ends of the wire upward and attach two washers to each end.

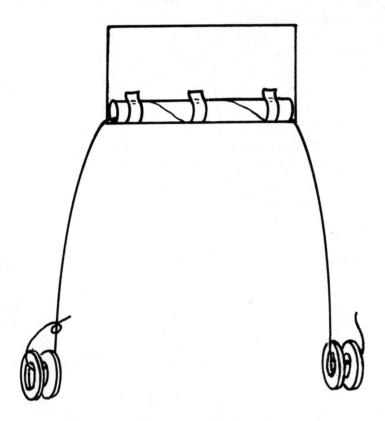

**7.** Make a loop around the washers at one end of the wire to represent the sauropod's head.

**8.** Press a piece of walnut-size clay on a table.

**9.** Stand the pencil, eraser end up, in the clay.

**10.** Place the model of the sauropod so that the straw sits on top of the eraser. Move the model left or right until you find the point where it balances.

**11.** Mark an "X" on the drawing at the balance point.

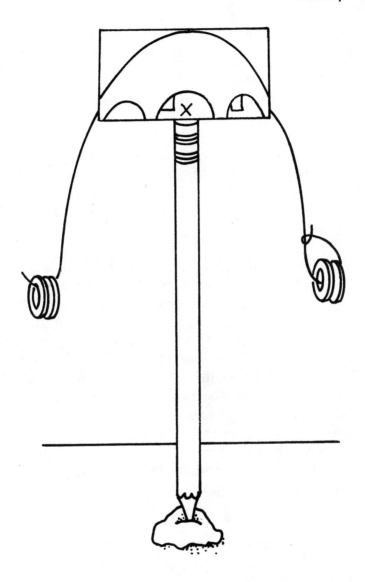

**12.** Move the wire through the straw so that about ¼ inch (0.6 cm) more wire extends from the neck side of the drawing.

**13.** Place the model back on the eraser with the balance mark (X) in the center of the eraser as before.

**14.** Observe any change in the position of the model.

**15.** Move the wire through the straw so that about ¼ inch (0.6 cm) more wire extends from the tail side of the drawing.

**16.** Again, try to balance the model on the eraser by placing the X mark above the eraser, and observe any change in the position of the model.

**Results** The model balances on a point near the center of the bottom edge of the drawing when equal amounts of wire extend from each end. When unequal lengths of wire extend from the ends of the straw, the paper tilts toward the end that has the longer wire.

**Why?** The point on any object where it is in balance is its **center of gravity**. In the model of the sauropod, this is the point where all its parts counterbalance each other. Placing equal amounts of wire and washers on each end of the model caused the center of gravity to be at the center of the bottom edge of the drawing. When more wire was extended from one end, the paper tilted to the end that had the longer wire because the center of gravity changed. Dinosaurs such as sauropods had very long necks so, without a long tail to counterbalance the weight of the neck, these dinosaurs, like the model, would have tipped over. The length of a dinosaur's tail and neck may not be the same, but the weight and length of the two counterbalance each other.

## Solution to Exercise

### Think!

• Tail 1 is short, thick, and straight. Bipeds had tails like this.

*The best body choice for tail 1 is C.*

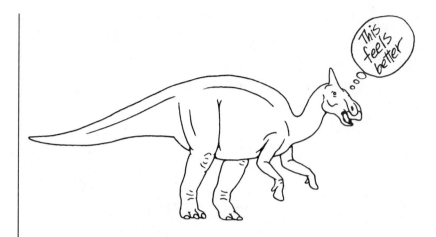

- Tail 2 is very long, requiring the animal to exert much effort to lift and/or drag the tail. Dinosaurs with very long necks usually had long tails to counterbalance the weight.

*The best body choice for tail 2 is A.*

• Tail 3 is armed with a macelike club on its end. Dinosaurs with armor-covered bodies usually had spiked or armor-plated tails.

*The best body choice for tail 3 is B.*

# 14
# Body Heat

## The Differences Between Cold-Blooded and Warm-Blooded Dinosaurs

## What You Need to Know

Until recently most scientists believed all dinosaurs were slow, sluggish, and **ectothermic** (cold-blooded). But now a number of scientists believe that at least some of the dinosaurs may have been agile, fast, and **endothermic** (warm-blooded).

Modern reptiles are cold-blooded, but humans, like you, are warm-blooded. The body temperature of an ectothermic animal changes with the temperature of its environment, but an endothermic animal maintains a constant body temperature, regardless of the temperature outside its body. An endothermic animal's inner heat comes from the food the animal eats, and one way it loses body heat is by sweating.

Some paleontologists think dinosaurs would have had to spend most or all of their time eating to maintain a constant body temperature from food energy. The large dinosaurs, if endothermic, may have eaten about fifty times their body weight in food each year. Unlike endothermic dinosaurs, ectothermic dinosaurs probably ate only about five times their body weight in food each year because much of the energy needed to warm them came from solar energy outside their body.

Another way the large endothermic dinosaurs may have maintained their body temperature is just by being big. Their size would slow down the gain or loss of heat to and from their environment. Because of this slow exchange of heat, any changes in temperature from day to night would have little effect on the dinosaur's body temperature. Such an animal might even suffer from overheating during exertion or warm weather and might cool off during hot weather by bathing, wading, or standing in cold water.

Some of the ectothermic dinosaurs may have had special physical features that helped them control their body heat. For example, the fossil remains of **Spinosaurus** (SPY-nuh-SAWR-us) show that this animal had long spines of bone projecting upward from the vertebrae. These spines are thought to have supported a web of skin like a sail. During the cooler part of the day, *Spinosaurus* could stand with its side to the sun and

COLLECTING HEAT

the blood in the "sail" would heat up like a solar collector. The sun-warmed blood would then carry heat through the animal's body. If the animal became too hot, it could turn the sail away from the sun or move into the shade.

COOLING OFF

## Exercises

**1.** Fred, an ectothermic dinosaur, is preparing to take his nap. Which side of the tree in the diagram is more representative of the environment that will help him maintain his body temperature after he has eaten his snack?

**2.** Andrew, an ectothermic **Dimetrodon** (die-MET-ruh-don), has decided to take a walk during the heat of the day. Which would be the better choice of trails to keep Andrew from overheating?

## Activity:  CHANGES

**Purpose**  To demonstrate how environment changed the body temperature of ectothermic dinosaurs.

**Materials**    unruled index card
pencil
scissors
thermometer
timer
adult helper

### Procedure

**1.** Fold the index card in half lengthwise.

**2.** Draw a dinosaur on one side of the folded card.

**3.** Ask an adult to cut two slits in the center of the other side of the card. The slits should be about 2 inches (5 cm) apart and slightly longer than the width of the thermometer. See the diagram.

**4.** Insert the thermometer through the slits in the card.

**5.** Read and record the temperature on the thermometer. You may have to pull part of the thermometer out of the card in order to read the scale. Be sure not to touch the bulb end with your fingers, because the heat from your body will change the temperature reading.

**6.** Stand the dinosaur card outdoors with the thermometer in direct sunlight.

**7.** After 5 minutes, read and record the temperature.

**8.** Stand the dinosaur card in a shady area for 5 minutes.

**9.** Read and record the temperature.

**Results** The temperature reading increases when the card is placed in direct sunlight and decreases when the card is placed in the shade.

**Why?** Ectothermic dinosaurs, like ectothermic reptiles of today, were able to regulate their body temperature by moving into and out of the sun. The higher temperature reading when the thermometer was placed in the sun indicates that the dinosaur's skin would have received more heat when the animal stood in a sunny area. The blood in the vessels beneath the skin would have warmed, raising the body temperature of the animal.

## Solutions to Exercises

### 1. *Think!*

- Because Fred is ectothermic, his body temperature is changed by his environment. How did Fred's snack affect his body temperature? The ice cream lowered his body temperature.

- After his snack, Fred needs to raise his body temperature. Which side of the tree is warmer?

*Side A, the side with direct sunlight, will help Fred maintain his body temperature.*

### 2. *Think!*

- The sail on Andrew's back acts like a solar collector. How could Andrew keep his sail from collecting solar energy? He could point it away from the sun or walk in the shade.

- On which path would Andrew's sail collect the least of energy from the sun?

*Path A would be the better path to keep Andrew from overheating.*

# 15
# Egg Hunt
## The Search for Dinosaur Eggs

## What You Need to Know

Although egg fragments had been found, no dinosaur eggs were identified for what they were until 1922 when a group of American paleontologists made the discovery in the Gobi Desert. Since many **Protoceratops** (pro-toe-SAIR-uh-tops) skeletons were found near the eggs, it was assumed that the eggs belonged to this pig-sized, parrot-beaked dinosaur. As many as 12 or more of the potato-shaped eggs with their rough, wrinkled shells were found together in sandy nests. The eggs, about 8 inches (20 cm) long, were laid in concentric rings in hollowed-out depressions in the ground.

PROTOCERATOPS

Dinosaur eggs have since been found in many different places around the world, including a hill in Montana that is now called Egg Mountain. On Egg Mountain, baby dinosaur skeletons were found huddled together in a nest near the skull of an adult. Was this the remains of a mother dinosaur who was watching over her young? The discovery of this kind of family unit was unusual, suggesting that this mother, and possibly other dinosaur mothers, did not leave their babies to fend for themselves. The discoverer of the remains, John Horner, named the dinosaur to which the skull belonged *Maiasaura,* which means "good mother lizard."

Horner found more nests and eggs, as well as young dinosaurs with well-worn teeth. The baby dinosaurs' teeth indicate that they had been chewing on tough plants. Either the mother

MAIASAURA

brought food to the nests for these young dinosaurs, or she led the babies out to eat, then herded them back to the nests. This seems to indicate some dinosaurs lived as families. There are many unsolved questions about the nests on Egg Mountain, including what disaster caused the deaths in what seemed to be a dinosaur nursery.

Weak joints, such as those found in a *Maiasaura* hatchling, indicate that it must have been quite helpless and needed its parent nearby. Scientists also look at the condition of the eggs found in the nests for clues as to whether the newly hatched babies were weak or strong. A nest full of trampled eggshells indicates weak hatchlings who stayed in the nest for a long time, tramping back and forth across the eggshell fragments. Babies that hatched with strong bones and joints did not stay in the nest long, and larger shell remains have been found in their nests. The nests of *Hypsilophodons* contain eggshells in one piece with just a hole in the top, whereas **Hypacrosaurus** (hie-PACK-ruh-SAWR-us) nests have small fragments. From these findings scientists assume that the baby *Hypsilophodons* were able to look for food soon after breaking out of their shells, but *Hypacrosaurus* hatchlings were dependent on one or both of their parents to bring food to the nest as they grew stronger.

## Exercises

Match the description of the hatchlings to the diagram of their more probable nest.

**1.** A completely helpless baby with poorly formed joints and bones.

**2.** An active, get-up-and-go baby with strong, well-developed joints and bones.

## Activity:   COVER UP

**Purpose**   To determine whether dinosaur eggs were laid in nests that exposed them to air.

**Materials**   masking tape
two 1-quart (liter) jars
measuring cup (250 ml)
tap water
marking pen
2 paper towels
2 rubber bands
cookie sheet
½ cup (125 ml) of sand-leaf mixture (made by
    mixing sand and leaves)

## Procedure

1. Place a strip of tape down the side of each jar.

2. Pour three cups of water into each jar.

3. Use the pen to mark the level of the water on the tape.

4. Cover the top of each jar with a paper towel and secure with a rubber band.

5. Place the jars on the cookie sheet and near a window with direct sunlight.

6. Cover the top surface of the paper towel covering one of the jars with a thick layer of the sand-leaf mixture.

**7.** Observe the water level in the jars every day for two weeks, or stop when one of the jars is empty.

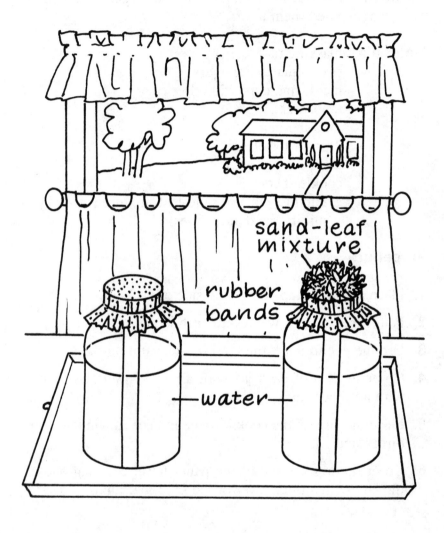

**Results**   The water level in the jar covered only with the paper towel is lower than the water level in the jar covered with the sand-leaf mixture.

**Why?**   The shells of dinosaur eggs, like the paper towel, contained many tiny holes. If the eggs had been exposed to air, their contents would have dried out. Because of the **porosity** (state of being full of tiny openings) of the eggs, it is believed that they were covered with sand and plants. This covering not only kept the eggs from drying out, but also protected them from predators and kept them warm.

## Solutions to Exercises

### 1. *Think!*

- What happens to the eggshells when the babies are helpless and stay in the nest longer? The shells are trampled by the babies and only fragments are found in the nests.

*Nest B is the more probable nest of the helpless baby.*

### 2. *Think!*

- Strong hatchlings break out of the shell and get up and go. These active babies leave the nest very quickly, thus the shells are not as broken.

*Nest A is the more probable nest of the active baby.*

# 16
# Oversized

## Dinosaur Egg Sizes and Shapes

## What You Need to Know

Scientists have found dinosaur eggs in different sizes, shapes, and textures. Not all of the eggs have been identified because some were not found near dinosaur bones. Two types of eggs that have been identified were laid by the *Protoceratops* in the Gobi Desert and the **Hypselosaurus** (HIP-sih-luh-SAWR-us) in France. *Protoceratops* laid potato-shaped eggs about 6 inches (15 cm) long with rough, wrinkled shells. *Hypselosaurus* eggs had a roundish shape and a rough sandpapery surface, and were about 10 inches (25 cm) long. *Hypselosaurus* eggs are the largest dinosaur eggs found to date, with an average content of 3.3 quarts (liters). Oval dinosaur eggs have been found, as well as some that are elongated with nearly pointed ends.

Surprisingly, the size of the dinosaur egg does not depend on the size of the parents. Some very large dinosaurs laid eggs smaller than those of smaller dinosaurs. The ratio of the weight of the parent to the weight of the hatchling of some modern animals that lay eggs varies greatly. In birds the ratio varies from about 4:1 in the kiwi to about 60:1 in the ostrich. Thus, if the adult kiwi weighs four pounds (1.8 kg), its hatchling would weigh one pound (0.45 kg). An adult ostrich weighs about 60 times as much as a baby ostrich. The ratio for crocodiles is nearly 2,000:1. This appears large until it is compared to that of *Hypselosaurus,* which is at least 10,000:1, or *Brachiosaurus,* which is as much as 100,000:1.

4 : 1

## Exercises

1. If a newly hatched baby *Hypselosaurus* weighs 2.2 pounds (1 kg), how much would it weigh as an adult if the ratio of baby to adult is 10,000:1?

2. If your weight increased between birth and adulthood at the same ratio as of a large *Brachiosaurus,* you would weigh about as much as a school bus by your first birthday. Round your birth weight to the nearest whole number and determine your adult weight using the growth ratio of *Brachiosaurus,* which is about 100,000:1.

## Activity:  TOO BIG

**Purpose**   To determine why dinosaur eggs are so small compared to the adult dinosaur.

**Materials**   1 paper towel

## Procedure

**1.** Hold the paper towel with both hands.

**2.** Stretch the paper towel slightly and place it against your mouth.

**3.** Blow through the paper towel. Make a mental note of the effort required to blow through the single layer.

**4.** Fold the paper towel in half and blow through the two layers. Compare the effort required to blow through the single and double layers.

**5.** Fold the paper towel in half again.

**6.** Try to blow through the four layers, and note how much effort it takes to blow through the added layers.

**Results**   It becomes more difficult to blow through the paper towel as the number of layers increases.

**Why?**   The shell of the egg, like the paper towel, permits air to flow through it if the layers are thin. But as the number of layers increases it is more difficult for the air to pass through. In addition, the liquid inside the egg exerts pressure on the eggshell. Larger eggs require a thicker shell to hold back the increased pressure from the inside. Thicker shells not only would have been very difficult for the baby dinosaur to break out of, but also would have restricted the flow of air through the shell. Thus, the thickness of a dinosaur egg, like any egg, is limited.

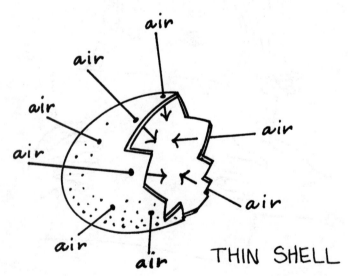

THIN SHELL

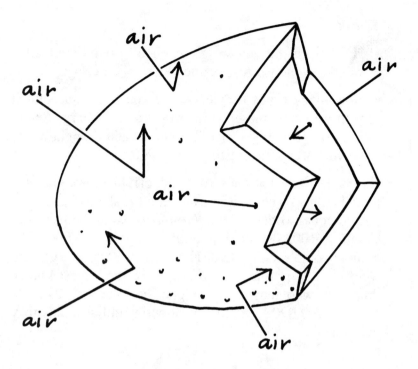

THICK SHELL

## Solutions to Exercises

### 1. *Think!*

- How much does the baby weigh? 2.2 pounds (1 kg).

- How many times heavier is the adult than the baby? 10,000 times. Thus, the weight of the baby as an adult would be the weight as a baby × ratio = weight as an adult, or 2.2 pounds (1 kg) × 10,000.

*The adult* Hypselosaurus *would weigh 22,000 pounds (10,000 kg).*

## 2. *Think!*

- How much did you weigh at birth? Round your birth weight to the nearest pound (kg).

- How many times heavier would you be as an adult if your weight increased at the same ratio as a large *Brachiosaurus?* 100,000 times. Thus, your adult weight would be your weight as a baby × 100,000.

**Example:** The author's rounded off birth weight is 7 pounds (3 kg). Her weight as an adult if she had grown at a ratio equal to that of *Brachiosaurus* would be her birth weight × 100,000, or 7 pounds (3 kg) × 100,000. The author would weigh 700,000 pounds (300,000 kg), and would be larger than the *Ultrasaurus,* the largest known dinosaur, who may have weighed as much as 240,000 pounds (109,090 kg) and was about as tall as a six-story building.

# 17
# Water Dwellers?

## Why Sauropods Were First Thought to Have Lived in Water

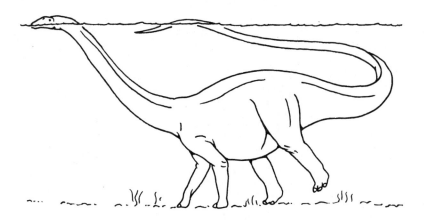

## What You Need to Know

Sauropods include some of the largest known dinosaurs. At first, the weight of these massive dinosaurs led scientists to believe that they could not have had enough strength to support their weight on land. They were considered **aquatic** (living in water) animals. Water would have evenly supported the massive weight of these animals, allowing them to maneuver around easily.

Nothing living today even remotely resembles a sauropod. Only their fossil remains give clues as to how they lived. Early scientists used the increase in height between a human and the dinosaur to estimate the strength and weight of the dinosaur. **Squaring** (multiplying a number by itself) the increase in height indicates how many times stronger the dinosaur is than the human. **Cubing** (multiplying a number by itself twice) the increase in height indicates how many times heavier the dinosaur is.

An example of this is the comparison between an imaginary sauropod called *Deanosaurus* (dee-nuh-SAWR-us), or "Deano" for short, and a boy named Tom. Tom is 5 feet (1.5 m) tall and Deano is 10 feet (3 m) tall. Deano is two times as tall as Tom, thus 2 is the increase in height. The strength of Deano's muscles is equal to the square of the increase, $2 \times 2$, making Deano four times as strong as Tom.

Tom                    Deano

Deano's weight is the cube of the increase, $2 \times 2 \times 2$, indicating that Deano is eight times as heavy as Tom.

If Deano is eight times as heavy, but only four times as strong, he lacks muscle strength to support his own weight. He needs help to lift his heavy body. A large crane would have been useful, but was unavailable during the prehistoric period. Scientists guessed that the best available support was water, and pictured sauropods such as Deano as wading and swimming in swampy areas and eating water plants. (For more recent scientific thinking about these dinosaurs, see the next chapter, "Land Dwellers?".)

## Exercises

Use the diagram to determine the increase in height between the young *Brachiosaurus* and the man. Use the increase in height to calculate the following:

**1.** How many times stronger is *Brachiosaurus* than the man?

**2.** How many times heavier is *Brachiosaurus* than the man?

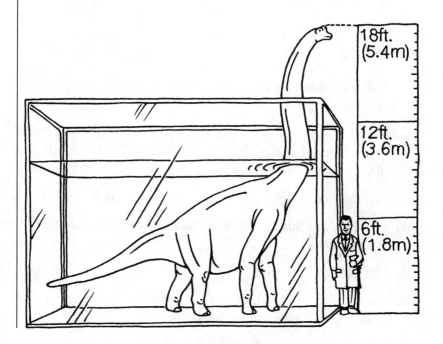

## Activity: LIFTER

**Purpose**   To demonstrate the uplifting force of water.

**Materials**   one 1-gallon (4-liter) wide-mouth jar
tap water
3 large rubber bands
ruler
masking tape
small bottle with lid (must fit inside
   wide-mouth jar)
permanent marker (NOTE: *Take care not to
   mark on your skin or your clothes.*)
poster board, 6 × 6 inches (15 × 15 cm)
scissors
string

## Procedure

1. Fill the wide-mouth jar three-quarters full of water and set it on a table.

2. Make a scale by securing the end of one of the rubber bands to the back of the ruler with masking tape. Flip the other end of the rubber band over the face of the ruler.

3. Fill the small bottle with water and secure the lid.

4. Draw a dinosaur that is about as tall as the small bottle on the poster board.

5. Cut out the dinosaur.

6. Attach the paper dinosaur to the outside of the bottle with the two remaining rubber bands.

7. Measure and cut an 18-inch (45-cm) piece of string.

8. Tie one end of the string around the top of the bottle and the other end of the string to the free end of the rubber band on the scale.

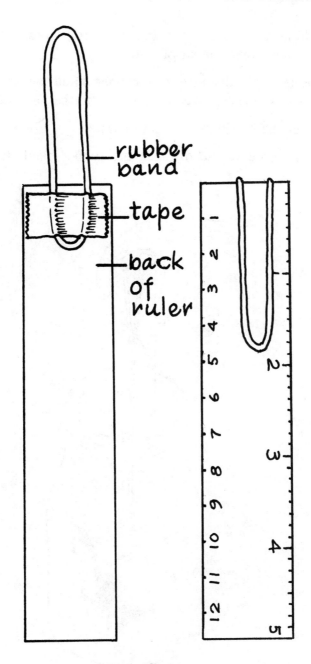

rubber
band

tape

back
of
ruler

SCALE

9. Holding the scale, lift it and the bottle so that they are suspended over the jar of water.

10. Observe the distance the rubber band on the scale stretches as the bottle is suspended in the air.

11. Lower the bottle into the jar of water.

12. Again, observe the distance the rubber band stretches.

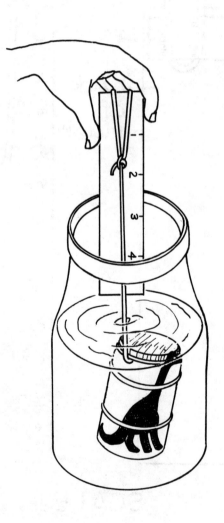

**Results**   The rubber band stretches a shorter distance when the bottle is in the water than when the bottle is suspended over the water.

**Why?**   The **weight** (the amount of pull that gravity has on an object) of the bottle changed when the bottle was placed in the water, but the bottle's mass did not change. The sinking bottle pushed water out of its way as it entered the jar. The weight of the water pushed aside is equal to the amount of lifting force on the bottle. This force, called the **buoyancy force**, decreased the effect of the downward pull of gravity, and thus reduced the weight of the bottle. The weight of large sauropods could have been reduced in the same way by the buoyancy force of water, allowing them to move around easily.

## Solutions to Exercises

### 1. *Think!*

- How tall is Tom? 6 feet (1.8 m) tall.

- How tall is the *Brachiosaurus*? 18 feet (5.4 m) tall.

- How many times taller is the dinosaur than the man? 6 feet (1.8 m) $\times$ ? = 18 feet (5.4 m). $18 \div 6 = 3$, thus the dinosaur is three times as tall as the man, and the increase is equal to 3.

- The square of the increase is equal to the comparative strength of the dinosaur, or $3 \times 3$.

Brachiosaurus *is 9 times stronger than the man.*

### 2. *Think!*

- The cube of the increase is equal to the comparative weight of the dinosaur, or $3 \times 3 \times 3$.

Brachiosaurus *is 27 times as heavy as the man.*

# 18
# Land Dwellers?

**Why Sauropods Are Now Believed to Have Lived on Land**

## What You Need to Know

Sauropods are a group of the largest known dinosaurs. Scientists used to think they were too heavy for their muscles to support their weight on land, so they must have lived in water, which helped to support them (see the previous chapter, "Water Dwellers?").

In recent years some paleontologists have decided that sauropods primarily lived on land and base their ideas on several pieces of evidence. For one thing, they have found deeply impressed fossilized sauropod footprints. The depth of these prints indicates that they could not have been made by an animal who lived in water because the water would have supported the animal, making the prints more shallow.

Other fossil evidence indicates that the **anatomy** (the structure of the body parts of an animal or plant) of the sauropods was more like **terrestrial** (living on land) animals than aquatic animals. Sauropods had pillarlike legs and short, stumpy feet like

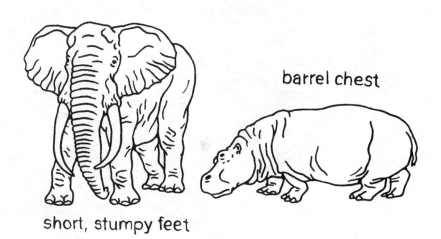

barrel chest

short, stumpy feet

those of modern elephants. The feet of aquatic animals are usually more spread out to help prevent their sinking in the soft mud and/or to act as paddles for swimming. The chest or upper body of a sauropod was also shaped more like that of the terrestrial elephant than the barrel-shaped chest of the aquatic hippopotamus.

The shape of an animal's tail also provides information about where the animal lived. The tails of aquatic animals are generally flattened on the top like a beaver's tail that moves up and down, or flattened on the side like an alligator's tail that whips from side to side to help the animal swim through the water. The fossils of sauropods do not show flattened tails, which also supports the theory that they were not aquatic. One additional piece of evidence that sauropods were terrestrial is that the fossil remains of these animals have been found together with fossils of other dinosaurs that were undoubtedly terrestrial.

The truth of the sauropod's habitat may be a combination of the early and recent scientists' beliefs. Some scientists believe these animals were **amphibious** (living both on land an in water). It is possible that sauropods spent part of each day walking around on the land, feeding off the tops of trees, and the remainder of the day wading, swimming, and resting in water.

## Exercises

From fossil bones, paleontologists can construct models of dinosaurs and determine the habitat of the animals. Study the three diagrams of feet.

**1.** Which feet most likely belong to an aquatic animal?

**2.** Which feet most likely belong to a terrestrial animal?

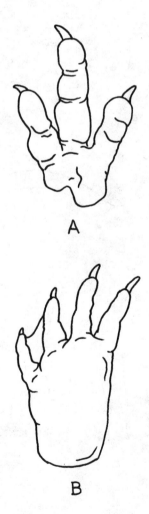

A

B

C

## Activity:  PADDLE FEET

**Purpose**  To show how a beaver's flat tail helps it move through water.

**Materials**  large baking pan about 4 inches (10 cm) deep
tap water
scissors
ruler
cardboard, at least 6 × 6 inches (10 × 10 cm)
rubber band

## Procedure

**1.** Fill the pan almost full with water.

**2.** Cut a 4-inch (10-cm) square from the cardboard.

**3.** Make a boat out of the cardboard by following these steps:

■ Cut a 2-inch (5-cm) square from the center of one edge of the 4-inch (10-cm) cardboard square.

■ Make the bow of the boat by cutting off two corners to form a point, as shown in the diagram.

■ Loop the rubber band over the end of the boat as shown in the diagram.

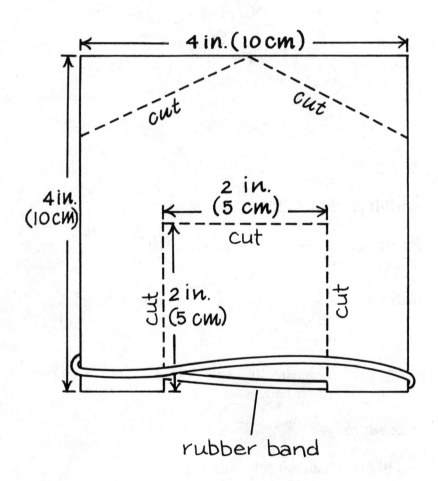

**4.** Use another piece of the cardboard to cut out a 1-by-2-inch (2.5-by-5-cm) paddle.

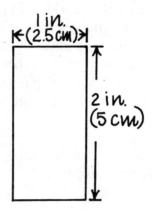

**5.** Insert the paddle lengthwise between the rubber band in the cutout section of the boat.

**6.** Wind the paddle by turning it toward you until you can no longer twist the rubber band. Hold the boat and paddle to keep the paddle from unwinding.

**7.** Place the boat in the pan of water.

**8.** Release the paddle.

**9.** Observe the motion of the boat.

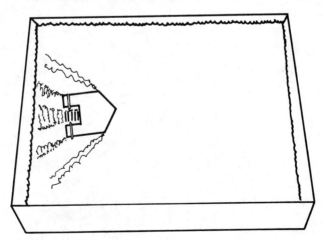

**Results** The boat moves forward.

**Why?** Newton's law of action and reaction states that when an object is pushed, it pushes back with an equal and opposite force. When the turning paddle or a beaver's flat tail pushes against water, the water pushes back, causing the boat or beaver to move. The flattened tail of aquatic dinosaurs, like the beaver's tail, were used to move the animals through the water.

## Solutions to Exercises

### 1. *Think!*

- What kind of feet do aquatic animals have? They are spread out, and some have webbing between the toes.

*B most likely belongs to an aquatic animal.*

### 2. *Think!*

- Do terrestrial animals usually have webbed feet? No, their feet are generally shorter and rounder than the feet of aquatic animals and some have claws.

*A and B most likely belong to terrestrial animals.*

# 19
# Track Record
## Using Fossilized Dinosaur Tracks to Determine the Speed of Dinosaurs

## What You Need to Know

Dinosaurs are thought by many people to have been slow-moving creatures. Some of the larger dinosaurs, such as the huge sauropods, may have moved at a speed no faster than 2 to 4 miles per hour (3.2 to 6.5 kmph). Others were very speedy. The **Stenonychosaurus** (Stuh-NON-ick-uh-SAWR-us) may have been the fastest dinosaur and could possibly have reached a speed of 50 miles per hour (80 kmph) or more.

Speed is determined by the distance traveled in a measured length of time. Because there are no living dinosaurs to time as they run, their speeds are estimated from fossilized tracks. The length of the **stride** (the distance from a point on one footprint to the same point on the next print made by the same foot) gives clues to the animals' speed. Another important

factor in determining speed is the length of the animal's back leg from foot to hip. Scientists can tell the dinosaurs with long legs because they have a longer **pace** (the distance from a point on one footprint to the same point on the next footprint made by the opposite foot) than animals with shorter legs. The longer the stride and pace of the dinosaur, the faster the dinosaur moved. The prints of modern animals are studied to give clues to the relationship of stride and pace to the speed of dinosaurs.

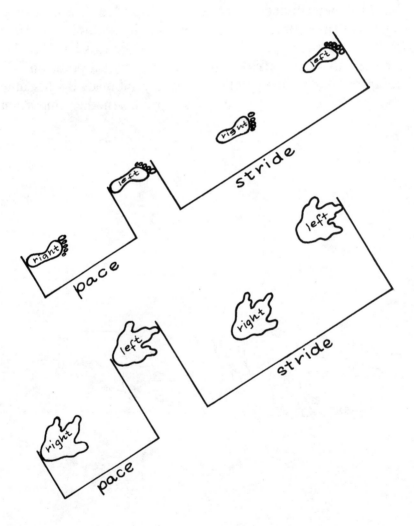

## Exercises

Use the two sets of tracks to answer the questions below:

1. If the tracks were made by the same animal, which set of tracks indicates the animal was running?

2. If the tracks were made by two different animals, which set of tracks were made by the animal with longer legs?

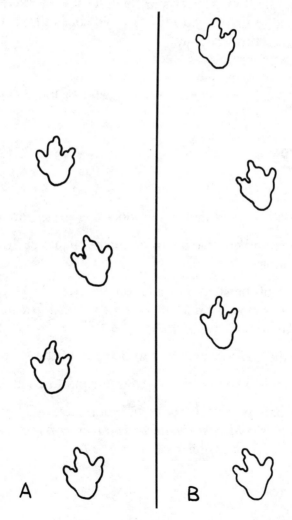

## Activity:   SPEED RACERS

**Purpose**   To use tracks to determine speed.

**Materials**   1-quart (liter) plastic pitcher
tap water
yardstick (meterstick)
scissors
butcher paper
shallow pan large enough to place your feet into
2 pairs of cotton socks (old socks that can be
   thrown away)
timer
marking pen
helper who has either shorter or longer legs
   than you

## Procedure

1. Fill the pitcher with water.

2. Carry all of the supplies outdoors to a grassy area.

3. Measure and cut two strips of butcher paper each 6 yards (6 m) long.

4. Lay one of the strips of paper on the grass. NOTE: *If the paper has a waxy side, place that side against the grass and the nonwaxy side up.*

5. Place the shallow pan next to one end of the strip.

6. Pour about 1 inch (2.5 cm) of water into the pan.

7. Put a pair of cotton socks on your feet. NOTE: *If the weather is cold, you should put on rubber boots and wear a large pair of cotton socks over the boots.*

8. Wet the bottom of the socks by stepping into the pan of water.

9. Stand at the end of the strip of paper and ask your helper to time you as you walk at a normal speed to the other end.

10. Record the time as your walking time.

11. Use the marking pen to outline the wet footprints on the paper.

12. Lay the second strip of paper on the grass as before, next to the pan of water.

13. Wet the bottom of the socks again in the pan of water.

14. Stand at the end of the paper and ask your helper to time you as you run to the other end.

15. Record the time as your running time.

16. Use the marking pen to outline the wet footprints on the paper.

17. Use the measuring stick to compare your stride and pace. Measure from toe to toe or from heel to heel.

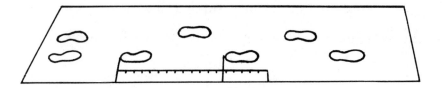

18. Repeat steps 3–17, with your helper making the wet footprints and you measuring the time.

19. Compare your stride and pace with those of your helper.

**Results**   The stride is shorter and the time longer for the footprints made by walking. The footprints made by running produce a longer stride in less time. The pace will be greater for the person with longer legs.

**Why?**   The sequence of the tracks on the paper is called a **trail** or **trackway**. Outlining the wet footprints with a pen produced a permanent print on the paper. Some of the prints of dinosaurs made in mud hardened over time and turned to stone. These fossilized dinosaur tracks, like the outlined tracks made in this experiment, can be used to determine the speed of the animal that made them. In this experiment, you compared the pace and stride of one person's prints made while walking and running with the prints made by a person with a different leg length. The pace of the person with longer legs was greater, and the stride made while running was greater than those made while walking. The same facts can be applied to dinosaurs.

## Solutions to Exercises

1. *Think!*

   • Which set of footprints indicates an animal was running? The faster an animal moves, the longer its stride.

   *Set B indicates the animal was running.*

2. *Think!*

   • Which set of footprints is made by an animal with longer legs? Animals with longer legs have a greater pace.

   *Set B was made by an animal with longer legs.*

# 20
# The End
## The Mysterious Disappearance of Dinosaurs

## What You Need to Know

About 65 million years ago, at the end of the Cretaceous period, the last of the dinosaurs died out. What happened to these giants who had ruled the earth? Did they die suddenly or over a long period of time? Nobody really knows the answers, but many scientists have studied the questions and many theories have been proposed.

Some of the theories are simple. Maybe other animals ate the dinosaur eggs, making the dinosaurs extinct over a period of time. Or maybe a sickness killed them off.

Most theories are more complicated, suggesting the presence of excessive radiation and significant environmental changes. Some scientists believe that a supernova exploded near the earth, flooding the earth with radiation for decades. Still others believe that many volcanoes spewed lava and ash into the air at the same time, resulting in a major change in the earth's climate.

More recently, scientists have proposed the theory that something from space, perhaps a meteorite, collided with the earth and destroyed the dinosaurs. This idea is based on the discovery of a thin layer of **iridium** (a mineral that is more commonly found in meteorites than on earth), in 65-million-year-old rock layers. This discovery led scientists to think that a large meteorite collided with the earth, creating a cloud of dust that encircled the earth for several years. The cloud blocked the sun's light and caused temperatures to fall, resulting in the death of both plants and animals.

Although this theory is supported by the discovery of the layer of iridium, it does not provide all the answers. Why did the dinosaurs become extinct while other animals, such as mammals, birds, and turtles, survived? Where is the crater that would have been produced by this collision?

## Exercises

The transfer of energy from one kind of living thing to another is called a **food chain**. Use the basic food chain diagram to select the best answers for the following questions:

1. What would happen to the other organisms in the food chain if the carnivore became ill and died?

    **a.** All of the organisms would die.

    **b.** There would be an increase in herbivores and a decrease in plants.

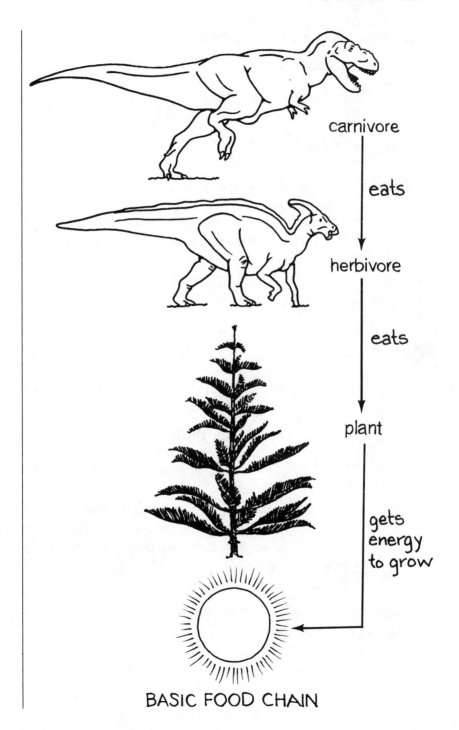

carnivore

eats

herbivore

eats

plant

gets
energy
to grow

BASIC FOOD CHAIN

**2.** What would happen if the sun's light was blocked?

   **a.** All of the organisms would eventually die.

   **b.** Only the plants would die.

## Activity:  **BLACK OUT**

**Purpose**   To demonstrate that plants need sunlight.

**Materials**   2 small house plants (of the same type and as similar as possible in size and number of leaves)
cardboard box large enough to hold one of the plants
masking tape

## Procedure

**1.** Moisten the soil of each plant with an equal amount of water.

**2.** Place one of the plants inside the box.

**3.** Seal all cracks in the box with the tape to prevent light from entering.

**4.** Place the boxed plant and the uncovered plant together near a window. NOTE: *If the soil of the uncovered plant becomes dry, water both plants with an equal amount of water. Open the box inside a dark closet and seal the box before leaving the closet.*

**5.** At the end of one week, open the box and compare its color to that of the other plant.

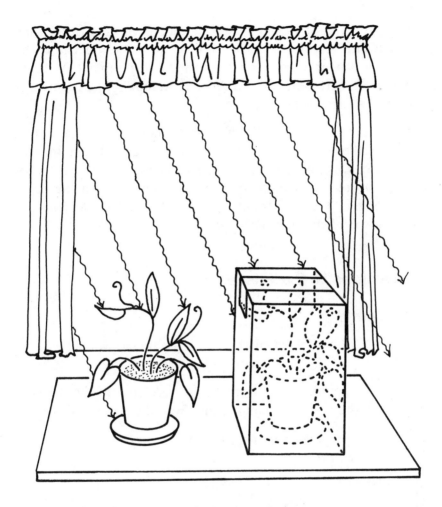

**Results**   The leaves and stems of the plant that has been kept in the dark are paler in color.

**Why?**   The paleness of the plant that was grown in the dark is a result of the lack of **chlorophyll** (a coloring substance used by plants in the manufacture of food). Without chlorophyll, plants not only lose their color, but their ability to produce the energy necessary for life. Given enough time, plants without light do not produce chlorophyll and will eventually die.

If the sun's light were blocked by clouds of dust from some cataclysmic event, the lack of light alone would cause the plants to suffer, as did the plant in this experiment. Without plants, the herbivores would die and eventually the carnivores would kill each other off.

This experiment has not considered other factors that would occur if the sun's light were blocked, such as a change in temperature. Design your own experiment to test the change of temperature that would result from a decrease in the sun's rays, or see "Ground Temperature" on page 132, *Janice Van-Cleave's Biology for Every Kid,* (New York: Wiley, 1990).

## Solutions to Exercises

### 1. *Think!*

- Without the carnivore to kill them who would be at the top of the food chain? The herbivore.

- If the number of herbivores increased, would they eat more or fewer plants? They would eat more plants.

*b. There would be an increase in herbivores and a decrease in plants.*

### 2. *Think!*

- Without sunlight, plants cannot live. Can herbivores live without plants? No.

- If the plants die, the herbivores die. Can carnivores live without herbivores? Carnivores can eat other carnivores, but they would eventually eat each other to extinction.

*a. All of the organisms would eventually die.*

# Appendix 1

# Dinosaur Glossary

**Anatosaurus** (uh-NAT-uh-SAWR-us, "duck lizard"): Many skeletons and several skin impressions have been found of this Late Cretaceous dinosaur. The presence of shrubs, fruits, and seeds in fossilized stomach contents indicates that this was a terrestrial dinosaur. Skulls indicate it had a thousand or more teeth and a keen sense of sight.

**Ankylosaurus** (ang-kih-luh-SAWR-us, "crooked lizard"): The body of this short-legged quadruped was covered with armorlike plates, and its tail had balls of bone on the end that were used to protect it from predators.

**Apatosaurus** (uh-PAT-uh-SAWR-us, "deceit lizard"): This dinosaur was so named because its bones were at first mistaken for those of the *Diplodocus*. It grew to be about 70 feet (21 m) long, and weighed about 30 tons (27 metric tons). Believed to have swallowed stones that were used to grind food inside its body. Formerly called *Brontosaurus*.

**Brachiosaurus** (BREAK-ee-uh-SAWR-us, "arm lizard"): A giant Jurassic sauropod that stood about 40 feet (12 m) tall, was 90 feet (27 m) long, and weighed 80–100 tons (72–90 metric tons).

**Chasmosaurus** (kaz-muh-SAWR-us, "opening lizard"): The holes through the long shield that stretched back over its neck and shoulders gave this dinosaur its name. Many fossils of this horned dinosaur have been found in Late Cretaceous sediments in Alberta, Canada. A herbivore.

**Coelophysis** (see-luh-FYE-sis, "hollow-form"): This small biped of the Late Triassic period had hollow bones like those of birds and is believed to have moved quickly to run down its prey.

**Compsognathus** (komp-so-NAY-thus, "pretty jaw"): This very small biped dinosaur (about the size of a chicken) lived in Europe during the Late Jurassic period. It most likely ate insects and small reptiles, and it is possible that this birdlike dinosaur had feathers.

**Dimetrodon** (die-MET-ruh-don, "two-measure teeth"): Not a dinosaur, but a pelycosaur, *Dimetrodon* had a great sail 2–3 feet (60–80 cm) long down its back that may have helped to regulate the animal's body temperature.

**Dinosaur** (DIE-nuh-sawr, "terrible lizard"): This name invented in 1841 by British scientist Richard Owen, was given to a special group of reptiles that lived from the Middle Triassic period to the end of the Cretaceous period. They existed for about 140 million years.

**Diplodocus** (die-PLOD-uh-cus, "double beam"): This Late Jurassic sauropod had a long neck and a whiplike tail. A complete skeleton has been found. Was 90 feet (27 m) long and weighed only about 12 tons (10.8 metric tons). It has broad pads on its feet like those of modern elephants.

**Dryosaurus** (DRY-uh-SAWR-us, "oak lizard"): Named because the top of its teeth had a shape similar to oak leaves, *Dryosaurus* was about 12 feet (3.5 m) long and 4 feet (1.2 m) tall, and weighed 170 pounds (77 kg). *Dryosaurus* had five-fingered hands and a small head with a beaklike snout, and walked on long, powerful hind legs.

**Hypacrosaurus** (hie-PACK-ruh-SAWR-us, "below the top lizard"): This large, hollow-crested dinosaur had a duckbill and was a biped. Fossil finds show that it was one of the most abundant dinosaurs of the Late Cretaceous period in Baja California. Fossils have also been found in Alberta, Canada. Hatchlings believed to be weak and dependant on one or both parents for food.

**Hypselosaurus** (HIP-sih-luh-SAWR-us, "high lizard"): This small sauropod of the Late Cretaceous period was best known for its large, round eggs that were found in craterlike nests in France—the largest dinosaur eggs ever found.

**Hypsilophodon** (hip-sih-LOF-uh-don, "high-crested tooth"): Many complete and partial skeletons of this Late Cretaceous biped have been found. It is believed to have been very swift. Although it had grasping hands, it is now believed not to have climbed trees because its fingers were too short to hold the tree branches and its feet were not adapted for climbing. Tail used as a counter balance. Hatchlings believed to be strong and left nest soon after breaking out of their shells.

**Ichthyosaurus** (ICK-thee-uh-SAWR-us, "fish lizard"): Not a dinosaur, but a marine reptile that gave birth to live young, *Ichthyosaurus* lived from the Middle Triassic period to the Cretaceous period. It is believed never to have left the water.

**Iguanodon** (ih-GWAHN-uh-don, "iguana-tooth"): This group of bipeds lived from the Late Jurassic through the Late Cretaceous periods, and probably lived all over the world.

**Kritosaurus** (KRIT-uh-SAWR-us, "chosen lizard"): A bipedal herbivore, *Kritosaurus* was about 30 feet (9 m) long and 15 feet (4.5 m) tall, and probably weighed about 3 tons (2.7 metric tons).

**Lystrosaurus** (lie-struh-SAWR-us, "shovel lizard"): A hippopotamuslike ancient reptile, this dinosaur had a jaw shaped somewhat like a shovel.

**Maiasaura** (mah-ee-ah-SAWR-uh, "good mother lizard"): This bipedal duckbilled dinosaur of the Late Cretaceous period was so named because it was found near a nest of babies in Montana.

**Micropachycephalosaurus** (MY-kro-PACK-ee-SEF-uh-luh-SAWR-us, "small, thick-headed lizard"): Only part of a skull of this dinosaur has been found, in Late Cretaceous rock in China. It is believed to have been a bipedal herbivore.

**Minmi** (MIN-my): Named for where fossils were first found—Minmi Crossing, Queensland, this dinosaur was armored with protective bony plates on its body and tail.

**Opisthocoelicaudia** (o-PISS-thuh-SEE-luh-CAW-dee-uh, "backward hollow tail"): A nearly complete skeleton of this Late Cretaceous sauropod was found in Mongolia. It held its short tail far off the ground. A herbivore.

**Parasaurolophus** (PAR-uh-sawr-AHL-uh-fus, "beside ridged lizard"): A Late Cretacean dinosaur of western North America, this duckbilled bipedal herbivore had an elaborate head crest. It was 30 feet (9 m) long and 16 feet (4.8 m) tall and weighed 3–4 tons (2.7–3.6 metric tons).

**Plateosaurus** (PLAY-tee-uh-SAWR-us, "flat lizard"): One of the earliest and largest dinosaurs of the Triassic period, this herbivore was possibly one of the first endothermic dinosaurs. A number of complete skeletons have been found.

**Plesiosaurus** (PLEE-zee-uh-SAWR-us, "ribbon lizard"): Not a dinosaur, but a fish-eating marine reptile that propelled itself through the water with powerful, paddlelike legs, *Plesiosaurus* lived during the Jurassic period.

**Protoceratops** (pro-toe-SAIR-uh-tops, "first horned face"): A quadrupedal, pig-size, herbivore, this dinosaur had a parrot beak and a small frill around its neck. Its potato-shaped eggs were the first dinosaur eggs to be identified.

**Sauropod** (SAWR-uh-pod, "lizard-foot"): These largest known land animals were so named because they had five toes like modern lizards. These herbivorous quadrupeds varied in height from 30 feet (9 m) to 100 feet (30 m). There were two groups of sauropods: those with peg-shaped teeth called the Titanosauridae, and those with spoon-shaped teeth called the Brachiosauridae.

**Spinosaurus** (spy-nuh-SAWR-us, "spiny lizard"): A large carnivore of the Late Cretaceous period, *Spinosaurus* had a huge fanlike sail or fin that stretched from the middle of the neck to behind its hips. This fin may have helped control the animal's body temperature.

**Stegosaurus** (steg-uh-SAWR-us, "roofed lizard"): This was a small-skulled herbivore with a brain the size of a golf ball, a spiked tail, and two rows of bony plates on its back. These plates may have helped control the animals body temperature. It lived during the Late Jurassic period, and many skeletons have been found in Colorado, Utah, and Wyoming.

**Stenonychosaurus** (stuh-NON-ick-uh-SAWR-us, "slender-clawed lizard"): A bipedal carnivore of the Late Cretaceous period, *Stenonychosaurus* was probably the most intelligent dinosaur. It had hollow bones, a large brain, large eyes, and slender flexible fingers. *Stenonychosaurus* was most likely an effective hunter because it may have used its large brain to equip itself with highly developed senses and fast reflexes.

**"Supersaurus"** (su-per-SAWR-us, "superior lizard"): The name is in quotation marks because it has not been officially described and named. Known only from a few giant bones found in Colorado, *"Supersaurus"* may have been an enlarged variation of *Brachiosaurus*. Found in 1972 by James A. Jensen, it was possibly 90 feet (27 m) long and 50 feet (15 m) tall; as tall as a 5 story building.

**Triceratops** (try-SAIR-uh-tops, "three-horned face"): The largest and heaviest of the ceratopsians, *Triceratops* is believed not to have had any real enemies. It was one of the last dinosaurs to become extinct. It most likely charged at its enemy like a modern rhinoceros.

**Troödon** (troe-o-don, "wounding tooth"): Small-size dinosaur at only 8 feet (2.4 m), but armed with long, sharp, serrated teeth and claws. May have had binocular vision.

**Tyrannosaurus rex** (tuh-RAN-uh-SAWR-us recks, "tyrant lizard king"): The largest and last of the giant carnivorous dinosaurs, *T. rex* was about 50 feet (15 m) long and 20 feet (6 m) tall, and weighed about 7 tons (6.3 metric tons).

**Ultrasaurus** (ul-truh-SAWR-us, "extreme lizard"): The largest known dinosaur, *Ultrasaurus* is estimated to have been more than 100 feet (30 m) long and 60 feet (18 m) tall, and to have weighed 120 tons (108 metric tons) or more. Only a few giant bones were found by James A. Jensen in 1979 in Colorado.

# Appendix 2

# Dinosaur Name Chart

Many of our English words are made up of root words from the ancient Latin and Greek languages. Use this list to help you understand what the dinosaur names mean. For instance, **Maiasaura** is made up of the root words *Maia* (good mother) and *saur* (lizard) so we know that this dinosaur probably took good care of its young. Try to figure out some names on your own.

| Root Word | Meaning |
|---|---|
| anato | duck |
| ankylo | crooked |
| anuro | tail |
| avi, avis | bird |
| bary | heavy |
| brachio | arm |
| caudia | tail |
| centro | midway |
| cephalo | head |
| cerat, ceros | horn |
| chasmo | opening |
| coeli | hollow |
| compso | pretty |
| di, diplo | two |
| dino | terrible |
| docus | beam |
| don, dont | tooth |
| dryo | oak |
| gnathus | jaw |
| hadro | large |
| hypacro | below the top |

| Root Word | Meaning |
|---|---|
| hypselo, hypsi | high |
| ichthyo | fish |
| iguano | iguana |
| krito | chosen |
| lopho | crest, ridge |
| lystro | shovel |
| maia | good mother |
| masso | bulk, body |
| mega | large |
| metro | measure |
| micro | small |
| minmi | Minmi Crossing, Queensland |
| nycho | claw |
| opistho | backward |
| ops | face |
| pachy | thick |
| pacro | ridged |
| para | beside |
| physis | form |
| plateo | flat |
| plesio | ribbon |
| pod, ped | foot |
| proto | first |
| rex | king |
| saur, sauro, saurus | lizard |
| segno | slow |
| spino | spine |
| stego | roof |
| steno | slender |
| super | superior |
| thero | summer |
| tri | three |
| troö | wound |
| tyranno | tyrant |
| ultra | extreme |
| urus | tail |
| veloci | speedy |
| vulcano | volcano |

# Glossary

Note: Refer to Appendix 1 for a glossary of dinosaur names.

**Amber:**   The hardened resin, or sap, from trees.

**Amphibious:**   Living both on land and in water.

**Anatomy:**   The structure of the body parts of an animal or plant.

**Aquatic:**   Living in water.

**Binocular vision:**   The ability to combine into one picture the images viewed by two eyes.

**Biped:**   Two-legged animal.

**Body fossils:**   Preserved remains of prehistoric organisms, such as bones or shells.

**Buoyancy force:**   An uplifting force, such as the upward force that water has on objects in it.

**Camouflage:**   A disguise caused by similarities between the colors and/or patterns of an animal's body and its environment.

**Carnivore:**   Meat eater; an animal that eats other animals.

**Cast:**   A solid reproduction of an organism that is made by filling a mold with a substance such as mud or plaster that hardens; a cast has the same outer shape as the organism.

**Cenozoic era ("recent life"):**   The fourth and present era of geologic time; began about 65 million years ago when the dinosaurs disappeared and has not yet ended.

**Center of gravity:**   The point on an object where it is in balance.

**Chlorophyll:**   A coloring substance used by plants in the manufacture of food.

**Continental drift:**   The theory that all the earth's land-masses were once one single body of land that separated over many millions of years and drifted apart to form what we now know as the continents.

**Cretaceous period:**   The last period of the Mesozoic era; 65–135 million years ago.

**Cubing:**   Multiplying a number by itself twice.

**Dinosaurs:**   Extinct reptiles that lived about 65–225 million years ago.

**Ectothermic ("outside heat"):**   Cold-blooded; the body temperature of an ectothermic animal changes with the temperature of its environment.

**Endothermic ("inner heat"):**   Warm-blooded; an endo-thermic animal maintains a constant body temperature, regardless of the temperature outside its body.

**Era:**   One of the intervals of geologic time based on changes in the earth's crust and life forms; the four geologic eras are Cenozoic, Mesozoic, Paleozoic, and Precambrian.

**Excavated:**   Dug out and removed from the earth.

**Food chain:**   The transfer of energy from one kind of living thing to another.

**Fossils:**   Traces of the remains of prehistoric animals and plants.

**Geologic time scale:**   An outline chart of the history of the earth divided into units of time based on geologic changes in the earth's crust and sudden changes in life-forms, such as the disappearance of dinosaurs.

**Geologist:**   A scientist who studies the history of the earth.

**Habitat:**   The place where an animal or plant naturally lives or grows.

**Half-life:**   The time it takes for half of the mass of a radioac-tive element to decay.

**Herbivore:**   Plant eater; an animal that eats plants or parts of plants.

**Imprints:**   Impressions made by organisms in soft mud that were preserved when the mud solidified; can be traces of an animal's activity, rather than its actual remains.

**Iridium:**   A mineral that is more commonly found in meteorites than on earth; a thin layer of iridium was discovered in 65-million-year-old rock layers.

**Jurassic period:**   The second period of the Mesozoic era; 135–195 million years ago.

**Mass:**   The amount of matter contained in a substance.

**Mesozoic era ("middle life"):**   The third era of geologic time; began about 225 million years ago and ended about 65 million years ago; often called the Age of the Dinosaur because dinosaurs are believed to have lived during this time.

**Molds:**   Cavities in rock made when organisms were totally or partially buried in mud that hardened into rock; over time ground water dissolved the organisms, leaving cavities shaped like their bodies.

**Nucleus:**   The center of an atom.

**Pace:**   The distance from a point on one footprint to the same point on the next footprint made by the opposite foot.

**Paleontologist:**   A scientist who studies prehistoric life on earth.

**Paleozoic era ("ancient life"):**   The second era of geologic time; began about 600 million years ago and ended about 225 million years ago.

**Pangaea ("whole earth"):**   The name given to the large, single landmass believed to have existed before the continents drifted apart.

**Period:**   One of the time intervals into which an era is divided.

**Peripheral vision:** The outer field of vision; what can be seen to the sides while looking straight ahead.

**Porosity:** State of being full of tiny openings.

**Precambrian era:** The first era of geologic time; began with the creation of the earth about 4.5 billion years ago and ended about 600 million years ago.

**Quadruped:** Four-legged animal.

**Radiation:** Energy released from atoms as they undergo radioactive decay.

**Radioactive:** The condition of elements that have undergone internal nuclear change or decay.

**Radioactive decay:** The release of radiation from an atom's nucleus; a change that creates an atom of another element.

**Relative age:** The age of an object or event as compared with that of another object or event.

**Retina:** The back layer of the eyeball, where images are focused on the eye's lens.

**Sediment:** Small particles of rock and mineral that are deposited by water, wind, or ice.

**Squaring:** Multiplying a number by itself.

**Stride:** The distance from a point on one footprint to the same point on the next print made by the same foot.

**Terrestrial:** Living on land.

**Trace fossils:** Tracks, trails, burrows, and other indirect evidence of prehistoric life.

**Trackway:** A sequence of tracks; also called trail.

**Trail:** A sequence of tracks; also called trackway.

**Triassic period:** The first period of the Mesozoic era; 195–225 million years ago.

**Weight:** The amount of pull that gravity has on an object.

**Zoogeography:** The distribution of different animal types throughout the world as a result of their natural movements.

# More Books
# About Dinosaurs

Benton, Dr. Michael. "Dinosaur and Other Prehistoric Animal Fact Finder." New York: Kingfisher Book, 1992.

Colorful illustrations showing what many of the more well known dinosaurs looked like. A dictionary of common dinosaurs with basic descriptions of appearances, habitats, and activities.

Berenstain, Michael. *The Biggest Dinosaur.* New York: Western Publishing Company, Inc., 1989.

Very easy reading, with large, fun, colored diagrams. The diagram of the Brontosaurus nursery is of particular interest. Art diagrams comparing the sizes of the tallest dinosaurs known to date give a better perspective of just how huge these animals were.

Berenstain, Michael. *King of the Dinosaurs.* New York: Western Publishing Company, 1989.

An easy-to-read book with many large colorful diagrams about one of, if not the most, famous dinosaur.

Berenstain, Stan, and Jan Berenstain. *The Day of the Dinosaur.* New York: Random House, 1987.

Very easy to read. Great art. In addition to the information that is given in a very simple way, the book is just fun to look at.

Craig, Jean M. *Dinosaurs and More Dinosaurs.* New York: Four Winds Press, 1965.

A dictionary about common dinosaurs in different eras. Helpful with the pronunciation of names. Large lifelike diagrams of each dinosaur.

Cuisin, Michel. *Prehistoric Life*. New York: Checkerboard Press, 1981.

Technical information including time before and after the presence of the dinosaur. Interesting section on the time scale of life.

Diment, Judith. *Animals of Long Ago*. New York: Macmillan Education Limited, 1976.

An easy-to-read fun fact book with many action-packed, colorful diagrams.

Elting, Mary. *The Macmillan Book of Dinosaurs and Other Prehistoric Creatures*. New York: Macmillan, 1984.

Excellent art and information. A particularly interesting section on the find of Lystrosaurus fossils.

Farlow, James O. *On the Tracks of Dinosaurs*. New York: Franklin Watts, 1991.

Farlow explains how dinosaur footprints became fossils. He describes how paleontologists study dinosaur tracks and use them to learn things such as how the dinosaur walked, ran, and behaved.

Fulston, Sylvia. *The Dinosaur Question and Answer Book*. Boston: Little, Brown, & Company, 1992.

Very informative book. Many remarkable questions that give you a new insight about dinosaurs. Great art. Interesting facts about dinosaur colors.

Harney, Susan. *A Dinosaur Directory*. Milton, MA: The Jacaranda Press, 1992.

A simple, easy-to-read directory about a few dinosaurs. A special feature is a diagram comparing each animal with man.

Harvey, Anthony. *The World of the Dinosaurs*. Minneapolis: Lerner Publications Co., 1980.

Basic question and answer book. Answers to commonly asked questions, such as "What was the biggest dinosaur?" Answers are brief, but thorough. Diagrams are colorful and interesting.

Kalina, Sigmund. *How to Make a Dinosaur.* New York: Lothrop, Lee & Shepard Co., 1976.

A simple to follow instruction book for making models of Stegosaurus, Brontosaurus, and Tyrannosaurus rex. These models are good for science fair displays.

Lauber, Patricia. *Dinosaurs Walked Here.* New York: Macmillan, 1992.

Great colored photographs of dinosaur tracks and on-site fossil finds. A section about dinosaur eggs.

Lauber, Patricia. *The News About Dinosaurs.* New York: Bradbury Press, 1989.

Helpful diagrams representing the behavior of dinosaurs. Interesting information about how some dinosaurs may have lived in herds, migrated, and cared for their young.

Norman, David. *Dinosaur!* New York: Prentice Hall, 1991.

An excellent technical reference of the complete dinosaur reign.

Norman, David. *The Illustrated Encyclopedia of Dinosaurs.* New York: Crescent Books, 1954.

An excellent technical information book. Detailed diagrams of fossil bones, photographs of actual fossils as well as colored drawings of dinosaurs represented.

Ravielli, Anthony. *The Rise and Fall of the Dinosaurs.* New York: Parents' Magazine Press, 1963.

Short, but packed with large realistic diagrams that stir the imagination. Interesting diagrams and information about the comparison of dinosaurs and their newly hatched offsprings.

Sullivan, Nora. *Dinosaurs.* New York: Franklin Watts, 1976.

An easy-to-read fact book about dinosaurs. Interesting information about the discovery of dinosaur fossils by people other than scientists. Simple diagrams of the more common dinosaurs.

Thompson, C. E. *Dinosaur Bones.* New York: Grossett and Dunlap, 1992.

Very easy to read. Simple, informative facts given with a question and answer section. Fun cartoon style art that makes learning fun.

Tweedie, Michael. *The World of Dinosaurs.* London: Treasure Press, 1983.

A valuable technical information book with great photographs of actual fossils and interesting colored diagrams of dinosaurs.

Wallace, Joseph. *Familiar Dinosaurs.* New York: Alfred A. Knopf, 1993.

Excellent pocket guide from the Audubon Society. Provides illustrated accounts of 78 of the most fascinating dinosaurs. Physical characteristics, location of fossil sites, and geological time period for dinosaurs is provided.

Warwick, Alan R. *Let's Look at Prehistoric Animals.* Chicago: Albert Whitman, 1966.

A general information book about life before and after the presence of dinosaurs.

Wilford, John Noble. *The Riddle of the Dinosaur.* New York: Alfred A. Knopf, 1986.

A technical information book, with some interesting black and white photographs of actual fossils. Gives the Who? What? When? and Where? of different fossil finds.

Wilson, Ron. *Dinosaurs of the Land, Sea, and Air.* New York: Modern Publishing, 1988.

Good general information book with simple, action-packed, color diagrams. A "Facts About Dinosaurs" list plus a glossary of dinosaur names makes the book especially helpful.

Zallinger, Peter. *Dinosaurs.* New York: Random House, 1977.

Short, easy-to-read history of the dinosaurs. Fun diagrams and an interesting section on different kinds of fossils found.

# Index

## HAVE MORE FUN WITH SCIENCE...
## JOIN THE SCIENCE FOR EVERY KID CLUB!

Just fill in the coupon below and mail to:
FAN CLUB HEADQUARTERS/F. Nachbaur
John Wiley & Sons, Inc., 605 Third Avenue, New York, NY 10158

Name_____

Address_____

City_____ State_____ ZIP_____

*Membership in the Science for Every Kid Club entitles you to a quarterly newsletter featuring science tidbits, games, and other experiments, plus other surprises...and it's free!!!*

✂ — — — — — — — — — — — — — — — — — — — — — — —

## More Exciting and Fun Activity Books
## from Janice VanCleave...

**Available from your local bookstore or use order form below.**

**To Order by Phone:**

**Call Toll-Free 1-800 CALL-WILEY**

__ ANIMALS (55052-3), @ $9.95
__ EARTHQUAKES (57107-5), @ $9.95
__ GRAVITY (55050-7), @ $9.95
__ MACHINES (57108-3), @ $9.95
__ MAGNETS (57106-7), @ $9.95
__ MICROSCOPES (58956-X), @ $9.95
__ MOLECULES (55054-X), @ $9.95
__ VOLCANOES (30811-0), @ $9.95
__ ASTRONOMY (53573-7), @ $10.95
__ BIOLOGY (50381-9), @ $10.95
__ CHEMISTRY (62085-8), @ $10.95
__ DINOSAURS (30812-9), @ $10.95
__ EARTH SCIENCE (53010-7), @ $10.95
__ GEOGRAPHY (59842-9), @ $10.95
__ MATH (54265-2), @ $10.95
__ PHYSICS (52505-7), @ $10.95
__ 200 GOOEY, SLIPPERY, SLIMY, WEIRD, AND FUN EXPERIMENTS (57921-1), @ $12.95

❑ Payment enclosed (Wiley pays postage & handling)
❑ Charge my ___ Visa ___ Mastercard ___ AMEX
Card # _____ Exp. Date ___/___

Name_____
Address_____
City/State/ZIP_____
Signature_____
(Order invalid unless signed)